JOTHIRLINGAM

JOTHIRLINGAM

The Indian Temple Guide

SURIYA

PARTRIDGE
A Penguin Random House Company

To order additional copies of this book, contact
Partridge India
000 800 10062 62
orders.india@partridgepublishing.com

www.partridgepublishing.com/india

Contents

Chapter 1

INDIAN TEMPLE GENERAL

TEMPLE CONCEPT:

Temple is an identity and meant for making connectivity between mankind and God. Temple means God's house. It is believed that murti inside the Garbagirah have potential cosmic energy within it, it radiates that positive energy always people whoever expose to that also receives that positive energy depending upon their receptive nature in their respective body. In some temple only mirror kept in Garpagirah that reveals greatest truth of ADVIDA (i.e oneness). God is in everyone. Whoever sees himself in that Miror will get a willpower and strength towards attainment of godliness.

The mirror kept behind the garpagirah reflects the Omni lingam as a many lingam. This gives greatest measage that living being all came from him and the same will disolved into Him when beings realize the non existance of Maya (illuson) in this material world.

T-TOLERANCE + E-ENRICHMENT + M- MANIFOLD + P-PURIFICATION + L-LEVITATION + E-ENLIGHTMENT

Which inturn helps the human being to attain the above.

TEMPLE COME INTO PRACTICE:

In Vedic period there is no built in temple seems to be. In Vedic period Yagasalai was in practice. Latter on in **Purana** period permanent in nature type temples were start built by Vedic followers.

TEMPLE BUILT TECHNOLOGY:

In olden days temple were built initially by using clayey soil, next by wood, next by using temperated soil walls, next by using bricks(they were built on Mayan principle as per sanga kallam literature in Tamil language and in Agananuru also explaining about destroyed olden days temple), next by utilizing natural caves, later on artificial cave temple, present days evidence of outstanding rock temple built available from the period **BCE. 273.** Onwards. The famous saint Appar descries in his Devaram about variety of temple such as Perumkoil, karak koil, nazat koil, kogudikoil, Mani koil and Aalza koil. The modern day temple has been built with RCC and stone structure and fusion of many cultures.

TEMPLE ARCHITECT METHODOLOGY:

HINDU temples were built in certain common principle across the country, broadly it has been classified into three categories they are.

   A. Nagara Architect (North Indian style)
   B. Dravida Architect (South Indian style).
   C. Vesara Architect (Fusion of north and south architect).
   D. Jain and buddist temples
   E. Islam and christian temples

Basic structure concept used in the Hindu temple is Square, Octagon and round shapes. All the kinds use the common principle such as tuvajasthambam(Gods Flag hoist post), Balipedam, deepasthambam, nirthamandaba, arthamandaba (or) anthralam Garbagirah, vimana(tower constructed on top of the garbagirah) and Prakara (Temple boundry wall).

Temple Structure has been co-related with human body parts as per below table:

Terminology	Meaning	Description
Paduka	Legs	Pillars used in temple for supporting structure.
Pada	Palm	Normally it is temple entrance
Jangha	Siren (shell produces sound)	Above the basement one part of the building
Gala	Neck	A narrow passage to connect big portions of temple.
Griva	Neck	A narrow passage to connect big portions of temple.
Sira	Head	Refer to base of temple santrum tower
Nasika	Nose	Nose like structure in temples
Sikhara	Hair	Refer to top most of temple santrum tower

VASTU WAS USED FOR TEMPLE CONSTRUCTION BASED ON THAT TEMPLE LAYOUT IS MADE AND PLANS DEVELOPED IN THOSE DAYS.

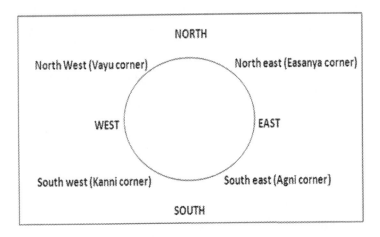

CIVILIZATION VERSUS TEMPLE DEVELOPMENT:

STONE AGE.

A. Paleolithic.   B. Mesolithic.   C. Neolithic

PALEOLITHIC (Early Stone Age)

the Stone Age began 500,000 to 200,000 years ago. The early part of the Paleolithic is called the lower Paleolithic and with the earliest stone tools dated to around 2.5 million years ago. Early Homo sapiens originated some 200,000 years ago.

MESOLITHIC (Middle Stone Age)

The Mesolithic period began at the end of the Pleistocene epoch some 10000 BP (8000 BC) and ended with the introduction agriculture. This introduction of agriculture period varies from region to region. The environment effect such as last ice age, delayed the coming of the Neolithic until as late as 4000 BCE (6,000 BP) in northern Europe.

NEOLITHIC (New Stone age).

"Neolithic" means "New Stone Age." This was a period of primitive technological and social development, toward the end of the "Stone Age". The Neolithic period saw the development of early villages, agriculture, animal domestication, tools and the onset of the earliest recorded incidents of warfare. In the *Neolithic* period did not fully develop metal-working technology.

AGRICULTURE PERIOD.

The Sumerians first began farming c. 9500 BCE. By 7000 BCE, agriculture had been developed in india and Peru separately, by 6000 BCE, in Egypt, by 5000 BCE, in China. About 2700 BCE, agriculture had come to Mesoamerica. The use of a specialized workforce by the Sumerians began about 5500 BCE. Stone was supplanted by bronze and iron in implements of agriculture and warfare. Until then Agricultural settlements had been almost dependent on stone tools. In Eurasia, copper and bronze tools, decorations and weapons began in about 3000 BCE. After bronze, the Eastern Mediterranean, Middle East, and china regions were saw the introduction of iron tools and weapons. The Protohistory period varies region wise based on metallurgy technology development in that region. For Sumerian region is as follows.

CHALCOLITHIC: (Copper age).

BRONZE AGE: (5500. BC).

IRON AGE:(3000BC).
HINDU PERIOD OF CALCULATION METHOD FOR LIFE CYCLE OF BEINGS.

Upto Ramayana Period is Trita yugam. Upto Mahabharat Period is Duwapara yugam **i.e 3102 BC** from this period **kaliyugam begins** *after death of Lord Krishna.* It is popularly held that the goddess of dharma represented as a celestial cow stands on four feet in **Krita Yuga**, three in **Treta Yuga**, two in **Dwapara Yuga** and one in **Kali Yuga**.

Brahama life period is 100 Brhama years = $100 \times 365 \times 4.32 \times 10^9$ Human years.

Ours 365 days equivalent to 1 day of Devatas.

Our 365 Years equivalent to 1 year of Devatas.

Devotas 12000 years equivalent to 1 sathuryugam.

2000 Sathuryugam equivalent to 1 day of Brahama.

2000x365 Sathuryugam equivalent to 1 Brahama years.

Krita-yuga = 4000 divine years, Santhya = 400 divine years, Santhyansa = 400 divine years. Total = 4800 divine years x 360 days = 1,728,000 human years.

Treta-yuga = 3000 divine years, Santhya = 300 divine years, Santhyansa = 300 divine years. Total = 3600 divine years x 360 days = 1,296,000 human years.

Dwapara-yuga = 2000 divine years, Santhya = 200 divine years, Santhyansa = 200 divine years. Total = 2400 divine years x 360 days = 864,000 human years.

Kali-yuga = 1000 divine years, Santhya = 100 divine years, Santhyansa = 100 divine years. Total = 1200 divine years x 360 days = 432,000 human years.

This equals 4,320,000 human years, or 12,000 divine years, in one cycle of the four yugas together, and 1000 cycles of these yugas equals a *Chaturyuga* at 12,000,000 divine years and 4,320,000,000 human years in one day of Brahma.

It is also explained that Kali-yuga began with the disappearance of Lord Krishna from the planet. This has been calculated to be 3102 BCE. Since Kali-yuga is described as being 432,000 earth years in length, with 5,000 years and more already passed, then the age of Kali-yuga has approximately 326,000 more years to go.

INDIA

Stone Age evidence

The history of India dates back to very old civilization Mohanjodara and Harapa which is presently in pakistan with the evidence of human activity and their relices presence. The Indus Valley Civilization which thrived in the northwestern part of the Indian subcontinent 5500 years before was the first major civilization in India and recent finds in Tamilnadu, before and after the explosion of the Toba Volcano indicate the presence of the first anatomically humans in the area. The tamil language is one of the oldest clasical language in the world. The Mahabharat description of *pandavas existence and Valmigi written Ramayana reveals the rich history of india.*

Bronze Age evidence

The Krishna presence evidence in the Gujarat state reveals Bronze Age in the Indian subcontinent dates back to around 3300 BCE. The upritis and tigeris river in present Iraq it is one of the worlds earliest civilization parallely exist in Mesopotamia civilization and Ancient Egypt during this period.

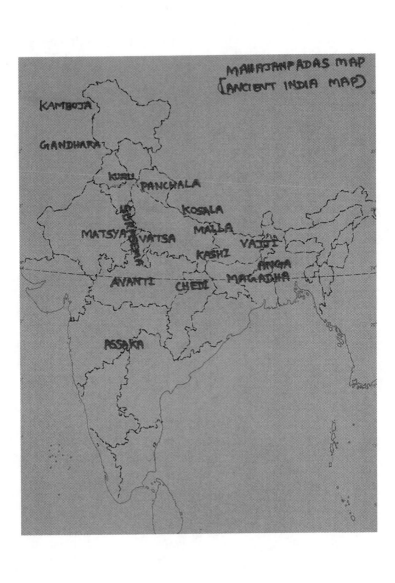

Vedic Period

The Vedic Period is distinguished by the Indo-Aryan culture which was associated with the texts of Vedas such as RIG, YAJUR, SAMA and ADARVANA Vedas sacred to Hindus, and that were orally composed in Sanskrit. The indain Vedas are one of the oldest texts, next to those in Egypt and Mesopotamia. The Vedas are the foundation and guide lines to Hindu civilization in india. The Aryans laid down Vedic civilization all over the North India, especially in the Ganges delta region. The present north western india excavation proofs(Uttar prdesh, Punjab, Rasthan and Gujarat) is the live example for Vedic period existence. The great Samrat Ashoka and king harshavardana made Nalanda university and Great Budhha existence inscription are the Historic evidence of later stage of Vedic period. The earliest Aryan were in india is represented in Rig Vedic, who appeared in the sub-continent about 1500B.C. They came in conflict with the Indigeneous inhabitants called Dravidians mentioned as Dasas in Rig Veda.

The INDUS valley civilization which spread across Present Pakistan and North western india. The relics of these civilization first discovered in Harappa in 1921 by RB Dayaram. RD Banjeerjee discovered Mohenjodaro in 1922.

Harappa civilization forms part of the Proto-History of india and belongs to bronze age. The Radio carbon dating reveals their existence from the year 2500-1750 BC.

Main worship of of these people was Mother Goddess, but upper class people preferred a god much similar to Pasupathi Lord Siva. Phallus (Lingam) worship was alos prevalent. However no temple has been found, though idolatry was practiced.

VEDIC LITERATURE

It elaborates knowledge over the subject of Socio-economic life of Aryans. These literature has been divided in to four parts as below mentioned 1. Vedas 2. Brahmana 3. Aranyakas 4. Upanishads.

Mahajanapadas:

This period saw the second major rise in urbanization in India after the vedic Civilization. The word Janapadas litteraly means the Land where the Jana(People) settled down. The word "janapada" means footprint of a people. Some more important Janapadas become Mahajanapadas. There were 16 Janapadas present during 600-321 BC. These sixteen "republics" or Mahajanapadas has been established, namely as follows

1. Kasi-Capital was present Varanasi
2. Kosala-Capital was Sharaswati
3. Malla-Capital was Kushinagar
4. Chedi-Capital was Shodivati
5. Vatsa-Capital was Kaushambi
6. Kuru-Capital was Hastinapur and indraprastha
7. Panchal-Capital was kampilya
8. Matasya-Capital was Viratnagar
9. Shursena-Capital was Mathura
10. Ashmak-Capital was Pathan
11. Avanti-Capital was Ujjain
12. Gandhar-Capital was Taxila
13. Anga-Capital was Champa
14. Magadha-Rajgriha and Girviraj
15. Vajji-Capital was Varanashi
16. Kamboja-Captial was Lumbini.

As per history the period in present practice.

Ancient Period : (BCE 2500-600 CE),
Medival period: (600 CE to 1750 CE)
Modern Period: (1750 CE onwards).

NORTH INDIAN STYLE:

In **North Indian style** temples Deity placed in a place called as **Antralaya** and above that tower constructed in beehive-shaped shikhara. The gateways are simple and modest.

Ancient Period: (BCE 2500-600 CE)
Example:

Ashoka architecture- Saranath and sanchi in madhyapradesh- **Period 273 BCE. Guptas architecture-** Vishnu temple at Deogarh (Near Janci in UP)-Period 4th to 6th century CE. Sanchi in (MP), Poomara (MP), Thigava(Jabalpur in MP), Natchna (Rajasthan).

End era of ancient period:

500 CE to 800 CE during this period Buddhas were built an Kudaivari Koil(in artifical cave temple made) and using by rock temple constructed. These temple were constructed based on Braamaniyam and samana religious types.

Medival period: (600 CE to 1750 CE).

In medival period the temple architecture were flourished all over the India and attains its peak.

Period 750 to 1250 CE in odisha.

(Ex. Jagannath temple in puri, lingaraja temple at bhubaneshwar and sun temple in konark).

Period 950 to 1050 in central India, Chandella generation built kazoora temple, cholongiar built Gujarat temple and the moothra sun temple and abumalai temples.

Rastra kudarkal Architecture- Kailasanathar temple in Ellora- 8thcentury

SOUTH INDIAN STYLE:

The pallavas were pioneer for this south Indian style architecture, latter on it was developed by cholas, pandias, and vijanagar and naiukkar kingdoms. In **south Indian style temples** Deity placed in a place called as **Garbagriha** on top of that a pyramid-shaped tower called **Vimana** was constructed. The gateways are constructed with highly ornate entrance called **Gopurams** were distinctive feature (The shore temple at Mahabalipuram and kailashnatha temple at Kanchipuram).

End era of ancient period:

500 CE to 800 CE, during this period, In east pallavas, west chaalukias, south Madurai Pandian were remarkable kingdoms developed and promoted this Kudaivari koil architecture.

Pallava architecture:

Mahabalipuram kodaivari temple is famous for this kind. Kailasanathar and vaigonda perumal temples in kanchipuram - **Period 700 to 800 CE.**

Medival period: (600 CE to 1750 CE)

Chola architecture - Prahgadeshwarar temple in Thanjavur and Gangaikanda cholapuram temple were built in 11th century.

Hoysalas architecture - Temples at Belur and Halebid.

Vijayanagar architecture- Hampi temple in Bellary near in Karnataka.

Vesara architecture: Somnath temple

Chaalukias kingdom:

Period 450 CE to 650 CE In western part of south india Aihole and Pattadakal type temples-Huchimalligudi, durgai amman and Ladkhan temple in Karnataka were famous for this kind of temples.

OTHER FAMOUS HINDU TEMPLE PRESENTLY LOCATED OUTSIDE THE INDIA

TEMPLE NAME	COUNTRY	PERIOD
Idong Songo (siva temple)	Java, indonesia	8 to 9th century
Lara Jonggrang	Pranbanan	9 to 10th century
Majabahid king built temple	Panatharan, Java	14th century
Kodaivarai mugafpu temple	Thambaksiring, balli	11th century
Annai temple	Baysak, Balli	14th century
Cen laa temple	Sambar ifree cook, Kombodia	7 to 8th century
Pandey sree temple	Angore, Kombodia	10th century
Angorewatt temple built by suriyavarman king	Angore, Kombodia	12th century

SHIVA AND KRISHNA EXISTENCE PROVED RECENTLY BY ARCHEALOGY DEPARTMENT OF INDIA RFER TABLE

SHIVA	EXISTANCE	KRISHNA
Unknown	Birth	Dwapara yuga around **30th century BCE**
Unknown	Death	Dwapara yuga
Unknown	Mode of death	Shot by a hunter
Celestial bodies	Locality	Vrindavan, Dwaraka
The moon and river ganga	Crown	Peacock feather
Hanuman, Veerabhadra, Ashwathama, Adi sankara	Avatars	Was himself an avatar of lord vishnu

TEMPLE SCIENCE

TYPICAL SIVA TEMPLE LAYOUT

West

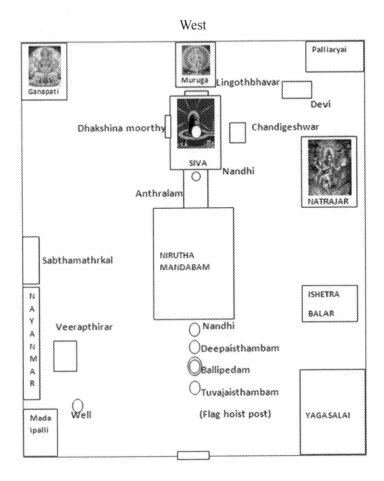

EAST

TEMPLE AND VIGRAGHA (deity) SCIENCE:

VIGRAGHA PRADISTAY USING SEVEN CHAAKRAAS PRINCIPLE

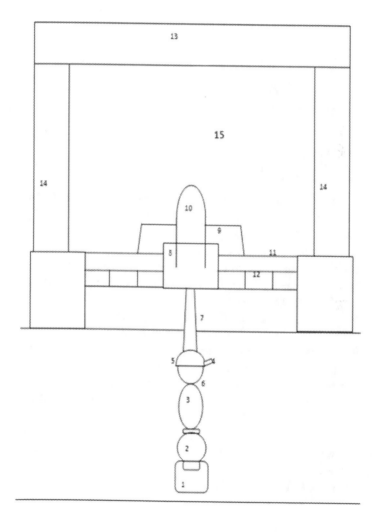

1. Aadharasilaa
2. Nidikumbam
3. Kal thamari
4. Kal aamai
5. Silver lotous and silver tortoise placed place
6. Gold lotus and gold tortoise placed place
7. Yoganaalam
8. Nabumsagasilla(Central Pedam)
9. Bedam
10. Vigragam.
11. Garbagirah floor
12. Istakaasayanam
13. Roof
14. Walls
15. Garbagirah.

Deity of gods were made based on description made in Rig Veda and latter on developed sastra description mentioned in palm leafs (Olyaichuvadi).

As per that **deity were made as three types**. Chalam type (moveable)-used for procession (Made up of metals). Second one is Aschalam type (Fixed type))-Used in Garbagirah (Made up of stone). Third one is chala aschalam-Used in Garbagirah as well as in procession (Made up of wood or metal).-Ex. Puri jagannath and Chidambaram Natrajar deity.

In temple **god was posture** in three methods. Isthaanakam-Standing Posture. Aasanam- Sitting Posture. Sayanam- Laying Posture. In general in Siva deity hands shows some muthra (yoga symbol), and reamaining hand consist with trisol & arrow. In Vishnu deity, hands consist with wheel, shell, kadai and lotus. Statue was made up of definite dimension ratio by applying THAALAMAANAM (Palm size) measuring method. Face size is – One time of palm size. Total deity size is – Nine times of palm size.

Types of Lingam:

Arida Lingam-The saint installed and worshiped lingam Divya Lingam-Devotas installed and worshipped lingam. Gana Lingam-Banarasuran installed and worshipped lingam. Manuda Lingam-The sculptures made lingam installed for worship. Suambu Lingam- The naturally formed lingam in river bed and in mountains.

TEMPLE AND SOCIETY:

The temple donation received from devotees was utilized for helping poor people, development activities, Annathanam (free food), free medical facility for poor people and to resolve the social problems and constructing chattiram (Like dormentry) to homeless people. In India different kinds of people held together by ahimsa(The same principle was followed by Gandhiji) and god exist in everyone's. This philosopy exhibits in temple by various sculupture in Gopurams, deity shapes and FRESCO paintings in roof and walls.

HINDU SACRED BOOKS:

The Hindu holy book is Prasthannatriyam. That includes Bhagavat gita, Brahma suitram and the other sacred book are Rig veda, Sama veda, Yajurvana veda, Atharvana veda, 18 Puransa in that 04 Vishnu purans and 10 Siva Puranas were famous one listed here they are (Siva Maha Puranam, Kurma Puranam, Macha puranam, Bowdigam puranam, Lingam puranam, Markendaya Puranam, Varagam puranam, Saiva puranam Vamana Puranan, iskantha Puranam) Bramanda Puranam Kalika Purananm, Brhama Puranam, Agni Puranam, Matyasa Puranan, Bavisha Puranam, Soura Puranam, Poovisa Puranam. Srimath Bhagavatham, Devi Bhagavatham, Siva leela Amrutham, Gurusarithiram, Devaram, Thiruvasakam, Agananuru Purananuru, Vishnu Puranam, Karuda Puranam, Ramayana written in Trita yugam,

Mahabharat written in Duwapara yugam, Bhagavat gita was written in first month in 3066 BC during **mahabharat war time i.e. 18.01.3066- 04.02.3066 BC.**

HINDU SEVEN MOTCHA ISTHALANGAL (SACRED PLACES).

In kiruthayugam the devotas used vasugi snake as a a rope to rotate to and fro the Mantra hills to take out Amrith from the Milk sea. The devotas pulled from one end and Asuras from another end of snake and churn the milk sea, as the process was going on as a byproducts so many comes finally the Amrith came. To have this Amrith conflict between Devotas and Asuras came the war went up for 12 years.

Whenever the Asuras try to capture the Amrith it fallen over on earth in few sacred places namely as follows

1. Ayodhya
2. Madura
3. Haridwar
4. Kasi
5. Kanchi
6. Ujjain
7. Duwaraka.

64 TYPES OF DEITEIS OF LORD SIVA CALLED AS ASTASTA MURTHANGAL LISTED IN THIS TABLE.

1. Lingam	2. Lingoth bhavar	3. Mogalingam	4. Sadhasivar	5. Mahasadha sivar
6. Umamaheshwarar	7. Somaskandar	8. Umesar	9. Chandira sekarar	10. Varusa Panthikar
11. Varusa Parudar	12. Pujanga lita	13. Pujangathirasar	14. Santhiya niruthar	15. Sadhaniruthar
16. Kaligathandavar	17. Ganga visormoonur	18. Tripurantaka	19. Kalyana sundarar	20. Ardha naresvarar
21. Gajan thagar	22. Juvara baktar	23. Sartula harar	24. Paasu mathar	25. Gangalar
26. Pitcha danar	27. Singa harari	28. Chandesa anugiragar	29. Dhakshinamoorthy	30. Yoga Dhakshinamoorthy
31. Veenatara Dhakshina moorthy	32. Kalan thagar	33. Kamarii	34. Eloguneishwarar	35. Biravar
36. Aapakottharanur	37. Vadugar	38. Shatira balagar	39. Veera Badirar	40. Agorar
41. Thatchakubankar	42. Gigaraa thagar	43. Satguru	44. Asuvaradar	45. Gajan thigar
46. Jalantravathar	47. Ragapathagar	48. Trimurti tripathar	49. Egapatha trimurti	50. Gowri vara Pradhanar
51. Sukrathanar	52. Gowri Lilatharar	53. Visaapa ranar	54. Karudan thagar	55. Brahmasira kandesar
56. Kurmasankarar	57. Machari	58. Varahari	59. Pradhanar	60. Rata bisahaparathanar
61. Sisha bavar	62. Sugasanar	63. Ganda tharar	64. Harirarar	

63 Devotees called **Nayanmarkal** who excels the Saivam Principle in India listed in the below table.

63 NAYANMAR LIST WHO EXCEL THE SIVAM PRINCIPLE.

1. Sundaramurthi Nayanar	2. Tiru Neelakanta Nayanar	3. Iyarpahai Nayanar	4. Ilayankudi Mara Nayanar	5. Maiporul Nayanar
6. Viralminda Nayanar	7. Amaraneedi Nayanar	8. Eripatha Nayanar	9. Enadinatha Nayanar	10. Kannappa Nayanar
11. Kungiliya Kalaya Nayanar	12. Manakanchara Nayanar	13. Arivattaya Nayanar	14. Anaya Nayanar	15. Murthi Nayanar
16. Muruga Nayanar	17. Rudra Pasupathi Nayanar	18. Tiru Nalai Povar Nayanar	19. Tiru Kurippu Thonda Nayanar	20. Chandesvara Nayanar
21. Tiru-Navukkarasar Nayanar	22. Kulacchirai Nayanar	23. Perumizhalai Kurumba Nayanar	24. Karaikal Ammaiyar	25. Appuddi Nayanar
26. Nami Nandi Adigal	27. Tiru Jnana Sambandar	28. Eyarkon Kalikama Nayanar	29. Tiru Mula Nayanar	30. Dandi Adigal Nayanar
31. Murkha Nayanar	32. Somasira Nayanar	33. Sakkiya Nayanar	34. Sirappuli Nayanar	35. Siruthonda Nayanar

36. Cheraman Perumal Nayanar	37. Gananatha Nayanar	38. Kootruva Nayanar	39. Pugal Chola Nayanar	40. Narasinga Muniyaraiyar
41. Adipattha Nayanar	42. Kalikamba Nayanar	43. Kalia Nayanar	44. Satti Nayanar	45. Aiyadigal
46. Kadavarkon Nayanar	47. Kanampulla Nayanar	48. Kari Nayanar	49. Ninra Seer Nedumara Nayanar	50. Mangayarkarasiyar
51. Vayilar Nayanar	52. Munaiyaduvar Nayanar	53. Kazharsinga Nayanar	54. Seruthunai Nayanar	55. Idangazhi Nayanar
56. Pugazh Tunai Nayanar	57. Kotpuli Nayanar	58. Pusalar Nayanar	59. Nesa Nayanar	60. Kochengat Chola Nayanar
61. Sadaya Nayanar	62. Isaijnaniyar	63. Yazhpanar		

1. Virusabaarudar	2. Ardhanaresvarar	3. Hariharar	4. Natarajar	5. Kaamari
6. Bhairavar	7 Thakshinamoorthy	8. Somaskandar	9. Pitchaadanar	10. Urthuvathandavar
11. Jalandiraasurasamharar	12. Lingothbhavar	13. Chandirasekarar	14. Uma maheshwarar	15. Viswanathar

16. Partha piraharunar	17. Kalakala	18. Agoramurti	19. Bhikshadana	20. Tripurantaka
21. Tatpurusha	22. Satyojata	23. Vasu	24. Gangathara	25. Vamadeva
26. Gouri prasada	27. Sadasivamurti	28. Ananda	29. Sukshma	30. Sivothama
31. Ekanethra	32. Ekarudhra	33. Trimurti	34. Srikanda	35. Sikandi
36. Bavan	37. Sarvan	38. Pasupathi	39. Ukran	40. Rudra
41. Bima	42. Esana	43. Mahadeva	44. Rudramurti	45. Manonmani
46. Santhya Nirtha Murti	47. Vajna	48. Sakthi	49. Dhanda	50. Dwaja
51. Sula	52. Ankusa	53. Gatha	54. Pasa	55. Kadga
56. Chakra	57. Kamadhokana	58. Chandesa	59. Kiratarjuna	60. Vidhyesvara
61. Murtisvara	62. Gajasamhara	63. Mahameruvidanka	64. Panchadehamurti	65. Aditya
66. Daksha	67. Sadasiva	68. Markendaya		

VARIOUS NAMES OF LORD SIVA LISTED IN THE ABOVE TABLE.

In the above table Sl. No. 28 to 35 called as Vidhyesvaras (8names), Sl. No.36to43 called as Murthiesvaras and Sl. No.47 to 56 called as Ayudapurushas

108 LORD SIVA ISTHALANGAL PLUS JOTHIR LINGA ISTHALANGAL.

(Where the nayanmar sang **THE RYHMES** those temples called as **Isthalangal**). First 11Nos. and last one are **JOTHIR LINGA** Shrines (Bold one in red in the table) and Remaining 107 Shrines from 12 to 118 Shrines in Tamilnadu are listed in the above table. Sl.no 12 to 16 bold one indicates **Panchaboodha isthalangal**.

1. Kasi(UP)	2. Devgarh (Jharkhand)	3. kethernath (Uttaranchal)	4. Ujaini (MP)	5. Omkareshwar maanthaathaa(M P)
6. Tharukavanam (Gujarat)	7. Somanatham (Gujarat)	8. Veyrul(Maratha)	9. Thriyampagam (Maharashtra)	10. Bimasankar (Maharashtra)
11. Srisailam(AP)	12. Knachipuram	13. Thirvanaikaval	14. Thiruvannamalai	15. Kalahasthi
16. Chidambaram	17. Thirukandiyore	18. Thirukovilore	19. Thiruvatigai	20. Thiruppariyalur
21. Thiruvitkodi	22. Thiruvazuore	23. Thirukurukai	24. Thirukadaore	25. Thiruvarore
26. Thirunallaru	27. Nagapattinam	28. Thirukkarail	29. Thirukovazi	30. Thiruvaiore
31. Vedaranyam	32. Thiruvayaru	33. Thiruppazanam	34. Thiruchutruthurai	35. Thiruvedickodi
36. Thirupoonthruthi	37. Thiruneyathanam	38. Thirumazapadi	39. Papanasam	40. Cheranmadevi
41. Kodakanallur	42. Kunnathore	43. Murupanadu	44. Sri Vaikondam	45. Rajapathi

46. Cherntha poomangalam	47. Thenthiruperai	48. Mylapore (Chennai- 600001)	49. Mylapore (Chennai-600002)	50. Salem
51. Susinthiram	52. Thirunandhikarai	53. Madurai	54. Thirunelveli	55. Kumbakonam
56. Thirumanachery	57. Nedunkkodi	58. Vellore	59. Thirvizimizalai	60. Thiruvidaimaruthore
61. Bhavani	62. Suratappalli	63. Thirukkarukavore	64. Thirukazukondraum	65. Kizaperumpallam
66. Thiruvenkadu	67. Thirunageswaram	68. Kanjanore	69. Alzankkudi	70. Vaitheeswarankoil
71. Katchanam	72. Keyranore	73. Kaveripakkam	74. Thirukodika	75. Thirupoonkoore
76. Tirukondiswaram	77. Peruore	78. Thiruverumbore	79. Thiruvilanagar	80. Panaiyapuram
81. Andankkoil	82. Sirkazhi	83. Thirupananthal	84. Odukatore	85. Thirumarukal
86. Myladudurai	87. S. Puthuore	88. Thiruchirapalli	89. Pazaore	90. Thiruturiore
91. Thirunedunkkalam	92. Sirarperunthurai	93. Thiruvadanai	94. Thiru Avalinallur	95. Virudachalam
96. Udumali	97. Ayampettai	98. Thiruvothore	99. Uthrakosamangai	100. Thirupoolivanam
101. Thirupyangili	102. Srivanjiam	103. Thiruvalansozi	104. Thiruppampuram	105. Thidtai
106. Kezuvathore	107. Chathalapati	108. Thirumangalakodi	109. Erode	110. Therisanangkopu

111. Thiruturaipoondi	112. Chempoonaar koil	113. Thiruchathamangai	114. Thirukkolamputur	115. Lalkudi
116. Thiruvakkari	117. Sangarapuram	**118. Rameshwaram**		

In Tamilnadu 108 Siva temple visiting consider as Fulfilling the all Siva temple visiting power, that includes two Jothirlinga shrines Kasi and Rameshwarm. There are total 274 Devaram Padal petra thalangal by NAYANMARKAL out of which 118 thalangal mentioned in below. In this total 274 isthangal 264 isthalangal in Tamilnadu remaining 10 isthalangal situated across India. This Tamilndau isthalangal listed as region wise in Tamilnadu as THONDAI NAADU, NADU NAADU, CHOLA NAADU and PANDIYA NADU.

PANCHA BOOTHA THALANGAL IN TAMILNADU:

(1) Neer (Water) isthalam-Thiruvanikaval in thrichy (T.N.)

(2) Agni (fire) isthalam - Thiruvanamalai (T.N.)

(3) Vayu (Air) isthalam- Kalahasti.(A.P).

(4) Ahagaya (Space) thalam- Chidambaram (T.N.)

(5) Mann (Soil) thalam- Kanchipuram (T.N.).

Chapter 2

JOTHIRLINGAM SHRINES

Whenever Adarma crush the society the lord siva appeared and demolished the Demon and vanish the evil deeds in the society. As per the devotees request he manifest himself infront of the Devot in Agni form and impart HIS energy in Jothirlingams and settled in them for ever. When you visit these holy shrines you can envisage this truth and realize the sense of HIS gracious presence their. It is my opinion whoever offered with gift of lord siva definetly pulled towards these shrines and enjoy HIS omnipresence in their life time. Believe me I never thought about jothirlingam shrines visit until 2013 end, I was rumbling with my daily routine activities until my left hand shoulder has got dislocated, I have been at rest in home for 10 days. These 10 days show the direction towards HIM and given a thought to write this book. Writing about great lord of course need some experience and HIS powerful grace. In early 2014, The almighty humble grace took me to three Jothilinga shrine without a ample money in hand and my physical condition not permitting me to travel such a long distance. Only you have to do is just think about HIM with deep conscious HE will pave the path towards HIM. This is my realized truth by reading this book I hope you will also blessed with HIS grace and experience the same, this is my humble request towards the ALMIGHTY.

Daily early morning with devotion make prayer by rhyming below slogam you will get peace of mind and good things happen in your life only you have to start, remaining things happen automatically.

Saurashtre Somanaatham Cha Sree Saile Mallikarjunam
Ujjayinyaam Mahaakaalam Omkaare Mamaleswaram
Himalaye to Kedaram Daakinyaam Bhimashankaram
Vaaranaasyaam cha Viswesam Trayambakam Gowtameethate
Paralyaam Vaidyanaatham cha Naagesam Daarukaavane
Setubandhe Ramesham Grushnesam cha Shivaalaye.

The slogam in Maha Siva Puranam explains the location of the jothir lingam shrines and its chronological order as the shrines came into worship practice as follows.

1. **Somanathar shrine in saurashtre in present Gujarat (Veraval).**
2. **Mallikaarjunur shrine in present simandra. (Srisailam)**
3. **Mahakalar shrine in Ujjain in present Madya Pradesh. (Ujjain)**
4. **Omkareshwar shrine in present in Madya Pradesh. (Omkareshwar)**
5. **Vaithyanath shrine in present Jharkhand (Deogarh in Jasidih).**
6. **Bhimasankar shrine in present Maharastra. (Bhimasankar)**
7. **Rameshwar shrine in present Tamilnadu. (Rameshwaram)**
8. **Nageshwar shrine in Present Gujarat.(Dharukavanam)**
9. **Kasiviswanathar shrine in Present utter Pradesh. (Varanashi)**
10. **Tryambakeshwar shrine in Present Maharastra (Nashiq)**
11. **11. Kedernath shrine in Present uttra khand (Kedernath)**
12. **Kushmeshwarar shrine in Present Maharastra (verul)**

TRAVEL GUIDE TO 12 JOTHIRLINGAM IN ALL OVER INDIA AND PUNCHA BOOUDA THALANGAL IN TAMILNADU

Origin Town	Temple town	God Name	Route	KM
Delhi	1. Kasi(UP) Varanasi Dt.	Visveshwarar, visalatchi	Delhi to Varanasi by train via Lucknow	**815**
1. Kasi(UP)	2. Vasuginath (JK) Deogarh Dt.	Nageshwarar	Varanasi to jasedi by train	**477**
2. Deogarh(Jarkhand)	3. kethernath(Utran chal)-Almoda Dt.	Bhagaeswar	Delhi to Rishikesh by train, Rishikesh to Gowrikunt by 250KM by bus, Gowrikunt to kedaram 14km by walk or by horse or by dolli.	**1742**
3. kethernath(Uttaranchal)	4. Ujaini(MP)	Mahakalar	Kedernath-Delhi & Delhi-bhopal-Ujaini by train.	**1298**
4. Ujaini (MP)	5. Maanthaathaa(M P) North Nimat Dt.	Omkaresh war	Ujaini to indore 65Km from indore 70 Km	**125**

Origin Town	Temple town	God Name	Route	KM
5. Maanthaathaa (M P)	6. Tharukavanam (Gujarat)Jamnagar Dt.	Nageshwarar	Deli-ahamedabad-Rajkot- by train or air, Rajkot-Okha by train, from Okha t-Duwaraka via Tharukavanam 15km by bus.	905
6. Tharukavanam (Gujarat)	7. Prabasapattinam (Gujarat) Junagutch Dt.	Somanath	Duwaraka-rajkot-Veraval by train, Veraval to somnath 5km by road	400
7. Prabasapattinam (Gujarat)	8. Thriyam pak (Maratha)Nasik Dt.	Thriyampakeshwarar	Veraval-Raykot-vadora- Manmad - Nasik by train, from Nasik – Thriyampak 30km by bus	800
8. Thriyampak (Maratha)	Verul (Maratha) Aurangabad Dt	Kushmesh warar	8. Nasik- Manmad - ellora bus or Nasik- Aurangabad train route from there 22km by bus route to Verul.	220
9. Verul (Maratha)	10. Bimasankar (Maratha)Pune Dt	Bimasankarar	Verul to bimashankar by bus, Bimashankar to Pune 120 km by bus.	270

Origin Town	Temple town	God Name	Route	KM
10. Bimasankar (Maratha)	11. Srisailam (AP) Karnool Dt	Maligarjunar	Bimashankar-Pune by bus from Pune to Guntur by train, Guntur to nandial by train, Nandial to srisailam 7km by bus.	**895**
11Srisailam(AP	**12. Sri kalahasti**	Sri kalahastiswar swami	Guntur-Gudur by train, Gudur to Kalahasthi 75km by bus.	**485**
12. Sri kalahasti	**13. Kancheepuram**	Eagambareswar	kalahasthi to Chennai & Chennai - Kanchipuram 65km by bus	200
13. Kancheepuram	**14. Thiruvanamalai**	Annamaliyar	Tindivanam-Geenjee	160
14. Thiruvanamalai	**15. Chidambaram**	Natarajar	Virdachalam-Jayamkondam	165
15. Chidambaram	**16. Thiruvanikaval**	Jambugeshwar	Kombakonam- Thrichy	183
16. Thiruvanikaval	17. Rameshwarm	Ramanathar-Pervathavarthini	Thrichy-Karaikudi	**239**

INDIA MAP SHOWING JOTHIRLINGAM ACROSS INDIA AND PANCHA BOOTHA THALANGAL

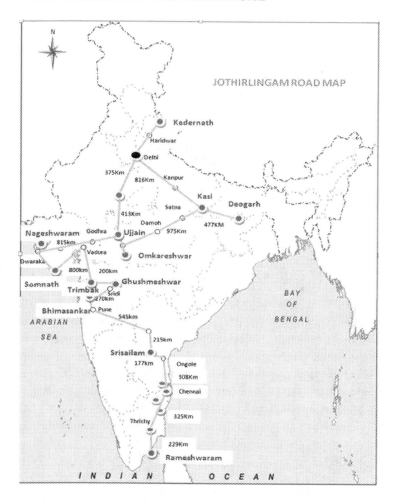

Red color dots indicate jothirlingam location.
Blue color dots indicate Pancha pudha thalangal in Tamilnadu.

Chapter 2.1

KASI VISWANATHAR JOTHIRLINGAM

KASI VISWANATHAR TEMPLE

God name – Viswanathar, Goddess name-Annapurani.

The temple can be approached from a lane called Vishwanatha lane. The temple is surrounded by many subsidiary shrines. A well called Jnana Vapi is also located to the north of the main temple. As one enters the temple from the southern side the first temple to the left of the pilgrim are three temples in a row one behind the other – Vishnu, Virupakshi Gauri and Avimukta Vinayaka. A cluster of five lingas enclosed in a temple is called Nilakantheshvar temple. Just above the Avimukteshvara Vinayaka are temples of Shanniswar and Virupaksha. To the right just near the entrance is the temple enshrining a linga called Avimukteshvara. There is a controversy regarding the original Jyotirlinga at the place, which suggests that not the Vishwanatha but the Avimukteshvara is the original Jyotirlinga.

It is also one of the Padal Petra isthalam of Vada naadu mentioned in Thevaaram. The temple is situated in varanashi the holiest existing place of Hindus, It is believed that a visit to Kasi ensures liberation & hence pious Hindus seek a visit during their lifetime. It is customs followed pour the remains of cremated ancestors ash on the River Ganges to liberate the Atma from their wordly bondage. Manikarnica ghat is the place where countless Hindus have been cremated. The kasi is famous for Devotas worship, Ancistor (Pindadaan) worship and Poodha worship. Varanashi got its name from two rivers, Varana and Asi flow here.

The temple stands on the western bank of the holy river Ganga, and is one of the twelve Jyotirlingas. It is the holiest of all Shiva temples. The main deity is known by the name vishwanath or *Vishweshwara* meaning Ruler of the universe. The temple town, which claims to be the oldest living city in the world, with 3500 years of documented history, is also called Kashi and hence the temple is popularly called Kashi vishwanath temple.

The lingam is placed in a square shaped brass plated pit. Devotees are permitted to offer worship such as abhishekam with holy Ganga water, garlanding the Lord, aarathi, etc. personally to the swaymbhu lingam. Kasi has got 11 nos. Swambu (naturally formed) lingas, Devotas installed 46 nos. lingas, Rishis installed 47 Nos. lingas, Gragahas installed 7 Nos. lingas, Kanangal worshiped 40 Nos. lingas, others devotees installed 295 lingas, the replica of other famous temple lingas 65 Nos. there fore all together 511 Nos. lingas you can see now also.

The kasi is famous for Devotas worship, Ancistor worship and Poodha worship. Kasi is amongst the holy spots for visit by the Hindus. It is believed that a visit to Kasi ensures liberation & hence pious Hindus seek a visit during their lifetime. This is the location of the Benares Hindu University, the place of learning of several aspects of Hindu culture. Here Parvathi Devi was so pleased that she offered food (Annam) to one and all and hence is worshipped as Annapoorani. The Lord himself is seen with a bowl in his hands asking for Annam from the seated Devi at the Devi's shrine adajacent to Viswanathar's shrine. This is considered to be one of the 52 Sakthipeedams (the place where Parvathi's left hand fell, when her corpse was cut by Mahavishnu's sudarsana chakram). After taking holy dip in Ganga the devotees take Ganga water and make Abishekam to lingam. By doing so it is believed the seven birth sins were purified.

TEMPLE BUILT

Kasi means light emission place. It has got 1800 temples comprises different discipline followed in Hindu. Kasi had very old historical things in it as per evidence the ARIYA'S who lived in this place 1400 BC. From Mahabharat also lot of references reveals about Kasi rulers. The ancient temple existance had been revealed in Mahabharat, The old temple had been destroyed several times by invaders, the recents temple was built in 1785 CE by Ahilyabai queen.

First attack: In 1193 the Afganisthan leader **Gori Mohamed** defeated the King Jayachandira and captured Kasi town. He destroyed many temple over here and built mosque on top of that, in 1194 he destroyed entire viswanathar temple Latter on the destroyed temples were built up whenever possible by Hindus.

Second attack: In 13th century the **Allaudin kilji** attacked this town and destroyed many temple here.

Third attacK: In 1447 due to other foreign people attack it was destroyed, again the temple was built ip.

Fourth attack: In 1494 due to other foreign people attack it was destroyed, again the temple was builtup. Latter on confidentially this temple has been kept and poojas were carried out regularly for 300 years. During king Akbar period, the pandit **RAJA PATAR got permission from akbar** and built the new temple with the help of **RAJA THODARMAL** and completed this temple **in 1585**

FIFTH ATTACK: In 1669 April month the mogal king Aurangasip destroyed this temple roofs, by utilizing the old temple pillars on top that the mosques has been built, this you can witness during your visit near to the present temple.

SACRED LINGA IN SECRET PLACE FOR 116 YEARS:

From 1669 CE to 1785 CE the linga had been kept in **Nanavabi well**, when Ahilyabai built new temple in 1785 the lingam has been taken out from here and installed in present temple by great her effort handsoff to her.. She also made arrangement for Lord Ramnathar to get Ganga water and Lord Viswanath to get Rameshwarm kodi theertham water for Abishegam purpose. Here the Garbagirah kept in one corner, due to special instruction received by people by **ASRI** voice during temple contruction time. As per sastra (astrology) norms **we should not make NAMSKAR to God here in Garbagirah, instead of that you have to make namaskar in Kukada mandapam. In 1839 the king of Punjab ranjit singh** offerd 30 Kg gold for Gopuram roof to cover with gold sheet. **In 1842** in the temple entrance, the NAUPATH KANA was built by **NAVAB ALI ALMULK** the ruler of kasi as per the instruction from British East Indian company first president **WARAN HASTINGS**.

TEMPLE HISTORY

In kasi the vishnu had created one holy well and continued his tabus there towards lord siva. Lord siva carry the Parvathi on HIS shoulder and made Kora thandavam, during this course the parvathi's ear ring fallen on earth. The Lord siva conveyed this message to the Lord Vishnu and asked him where about her ear ring. The Vishnu shows this holy well may be in this available. While Lord siva bowed and look at the well his ear ring (kundalam) also fallen into that. Upon lord siva departure from there with powerful illumination lingam has came out from the well. It is believed that both of them ear ring would have converted as lingam. Hence this lingam has been considered as Arthanarishwarar (Combination shape of parvathi and ishwar). The Lord vishnu took this illuminating lingam from there and installed in sacred place and made regular pooja to this and continued his Tabus there. Lord Siva inspired by Lord Vishnu's tabus towrds HIM. HE shown his VISWARUPAM to HIM(vishnu) and ask HIS desire. The Lord vishnu requested HIM to settle in this jothirlingam and bless all of these world being from here, whoever come to this place with strong devotion, ther sin to be melted down and to be purified person by taking bath in this holy Ganga. The Lord Siva considered HIS request and continuing HIS bless to all of us from here.

PUNIYA THEERTHAMS

The temple adjacent located **Nanavabi** called in many names as Siva theertham, Nana theertham, tharaga theertham and Motcha theertham. It is believed lord siva in water form in this theertham. The ganga river has got 64 Ghats in its bank here, out of that the Five Ghats are famous for taking holy bath and MAKING pooja for ancestor called as PITHRUKARIYAM they are Asi Ganga ghat, Thasatchva medam ghat, Varana Ganga ghat, Manikarnika ghat.

Don't miss to have bath in sacret ganga in your lifetime. Kasi is famous for Ganga holy bath it has got various ISNANA places to take a holy bath, for going to that places boats (thoni) are available. During your visit take a holy bath in below mentioned ISNANA stages in order wise.

1. Asi stage
2. Tulusidas stage
3. Anuman stage (where you can find tamil pandit more).
4. Harichandra stage
5. Kedara stage
6. Annapurna stage
7. Dasaaswamedha stage
8. Manikarnika stage
9. Panchaganga stage
10. Varuna

Apart from above the other stages are Janaki, Sivaala, Prayana, Thiruluchana, Meera and Pragalatha stages are available with nicely made steps along the river banks to take a holy bath.

CEREMONY

CLASSICAL GANGA AARTHI PERFORMED BY TEAM

Daily at evening at 6 PM the Aarthi taking at Ganga is wonderful ritual practice followed here, spare your time there. For Lord viswanathar 6 times pooja's were carried out in a day. In that the early morning bhasm Abiseka and night 8 o clock carrying out Sabtharishi pooja one must see without fail. The Dhandapani murthi who is sitting with stick in Nanavabi noth entrance gets first pooja, then only Viswanathar gets pooja this is the tradation followed here. Finally people before leave from kasi gets permission from Kala Biravar then only proceed to home town.

A TILTING TEMPLE IN THE GANAGA BANKS

Temple is full of heavily guarded with policemen. You can see the mosque in the picture adjacent to the main temple. The platform on which the original temple existed can be witnessed when you watch. The domes covered with gold were donated by Maharaja Ranjit Singh. Every ghat is named after the person who made it. You see Prayag Ghat – Queen of Putiya State.

PUJA TIME AND PROCEDURE:

The temple is kept open from 5.30 in the morning and stays so till 12 in the noon. The temple usually remains closed during the noon hours, and reopens in the evening at 4 p.m. The temple closes in the night after the last pujas are performed by 8 p.m. The pilgrims visit the temple any time of the day and worship the Lord by offering flowers and vilva leaves and chanting mantras of Shiva. The evening Aarati is known as Shringar Aarati. During this Aarati the linga is decorated with variety of flowers.

The temple boasts of a mandapa and a sanctum. A linga made of black stone is well placed in the center of the floor in a square silver altar inside the sanctum. The interior is not very extensive. Pilgrims come here to perform abhishekam to the pious Jotirlingam with holy Ganges water. Pilgrims can pay homage to the Lord at any time of the day. The Dhandapani murthi who is sitting with stick in Nanavabi noth entrance gets first pooja, then only Viswanathar gets pooja this is the tradation followed here. Finally people before leave from kasi gets permission from Kala Biravar then only proceed to home town.

OTHER PLACES TO SEE

In kasi other famous temples are Madhavarahi, Annapurani in this temple Deepavali featival carried out grandly wih charot made up of loddu, after end of the season almost at midnight, the luddu's from the charot is distributed to devotees. Sakshi ganaesha, Dundi ganesha, visalatchi temple, Manasa mandir, Khushmanda durga mandir, Kamakoteshwar temple, Kanchi kamakodi mut, kedariswarar temple renovated by Kumara kurupa swamigal here the boarding/lodging are provided for south indians, Sirungeri mut, Varahi amman temple, apart from that kasi has got 12 types of TUVAADHASA JOTHIRLINGAMS in different location they are

Kedariswarar-Omkariswarar-Vathiya natheswarar

Krishnaiswarar-Nageshwarar-Mahakalashwarar

Bageshwarar-Thirayambageshwarar-Shylashwarar

Kakarneshwarar-Ramaeshwarar-Visveshwarar.

There is a famous saint saying :

Having birth in Thiruvarur ledas to Mukthi.

Living in Kanchi leads to Mukthi.

Remembering Thiruvannamali Arunachalasewarar leads to Mukthi.

Fasting in Narmada river banks leads to Mukthi.

Death takes place in Kasi leads to Mukthi. Most of the Hindus prefered to die in Kasi to have a Mukthi.

END OF CHAPTER 2.1.

Chapter 2.2

VAIDYANATH JOTHIRLINGAM

2. VAIDYANATH. God Name-Vaidyanath, Goddess Name- Jaya Durga

VAIDYANATH

NAULACK

BALANANDA

TEMPLE BUILT:

This temple is one of the Sakthi Peedam too. The Devis heart fallen hence this palce(the place where Parvathi's HEART fell, when her corpse was cut by Mahavishnu's sudarsana chakram). Here the devotees Rhyms as **Jai Sambhoo, Jai Sambhoo Siva shankra shankara Jai Sambhoo.**

The **Ravana bulit the ancient temple during Ramayana period** and it has been named in the name of hunter as Pijunath who made regular Pooja to this lingam. Latter on this name has been converted as Vaidyanath in practice. The Mouriya and Gupta kings maintained this temple well in those days. The main lingam his 11" height. The top of the Siva Lingam is slightly bent.

SCUPLTURE WORK IN THE TEMPLE

The temple structure has a great amount of woodwork. The main sabha mandapam has several huge (wide as well as tall) pillars. There are twenty one Shrines in its premises. Direct opposite to Shiva Shankar Baba Parvati and Bhagavathi maaka shrine is there. Start from south main entrance the Chandrakup theerth is there, adjacent to that clock wise

1. Lakshmi narana
2. Sanniswar
3. Narmadeshwar baba
4. Durga Maa
5. Parvathi and Bhagavati
6. Ganesh
7. Bramaha
8. Gayatri maa (Veda mada)
9. Bairav baba (Mahakal baba)
10. Bajarangbali
11. Mansa maa
12. Saraswati maa
13. Suraj narayan bhagavan
14. Bhagala maa

15. Sri Ram chandar
16. Ananda Bairav
17. Ganga maa
18. Tripuri maa
19. Maa Tara
20. Maa kali
21. Anapurana Maa

Shrines were located among these temple in the center the Baidyanath is giving HIS darsan in Garbagirah as a Jothirling, the Singar Decoration is beautiful, you should not miss it. The locals call Baidiyanath as Ravanaeshwar. In Garbagirah no bags allowed only the Ganga gel or Chandrakup theerth water allowed for God offering. In this Baidyanath temple the three Nandhi's is positioned adjacent side with respect to Shiv baba, outside the Garbagirah. Instead of Nandhi the square shaped peedam was infront to the shiva baba while entering the main shine Pragaram. In this peedam the Agar bhakthi and other offering offered to Shiv Baba.

JOURNEY TO THE TEMPLE.

Get into the Delhi-Howarh-Chennai train and alight at Jasidih station from their 8 km by road you can reach deogarh temple. Nearst airport Patna than Calcutta. By train from Jamshedpur(277km), From Howarah(280km), From Patna(180km) and from Asonsol (60km) only. local trains available for Asonsol to Jasidih railway station. The Jasidih eventhough its is a normal junction but quit buzy even at late night hours. The pilgrims who goes to deogarh may utilize the clock room facility available at the station, keep your all bags in the clock room or lodge available at Deogarh. From Jamshedpur the steel plant spreads upto Asonsol the remarkable one is Bhranpur IISCO Steel plant located near by Damodar river, the Damodar valley in Asonsol where the Hydro power plant is there. The train strated from Jharkhand travel through west Bengal upto 70% distance again the jharkand strats just 30 km ahead from Jasidih junction. From jasidih to Deogarh 8 km local train /auto facility available frequently.

The devotees first go to Siva ganga theertham takes their holy bath here than proceed through south main entrance at the entrance itself the holy theertham Chandrukup is there where holy theertham water taken for god offering in morning Pooja time.

The Jothir lingam temple opens from morning 4 o clock and closes at 03:30pm and reopens at evening 7 0 clock. During shavan month lot of thousands of devotees bring their Kavadi, to send the devotees in controlled manure elevated corridor is made around the temple, from that corridor entire temple can be viewed nicely.

ISTHALAM HISTORY

The Ravanan king to get stable pleasure life, to become stornger than all and not to be destroy him by any warior in this world. To get the aforesaid, he made penance towards Lord siva and chant the Lord Siva Mantras for **10 crores times** finally he decided to cut his left out one head also, whilst the Almighty appeared revived him by putting his heads back in place, and offered him the boon of his desire. Because of this role of Siva as a healer, as a physician, he came to be called Vaidyanath (Vaidyan - physician).

The Ravana want to test his power as per Saint Narda Advice he try to remove Kailayam hills and shift the same to srilanga. It had created lot of shake to kailaya hills due to that the Devi and lord siva were got disturbed and cursed Ravana as your hands wil be get cut by one of my of Mahapurush going to get Avatar in this world soon. The lord by his left leg thump finger pressed the kailayam hill to settle back. The Ravana hands trapped in the bottom of the hill. As per **Vagesa saint** advice the Ravana sang the Samaveda by hearing his nice **Samaveda ryhmes** lord siva got pleasure mode and rscued the Ravana from this tragedy. Upon hearing his statement in the desire to keep HIM in lanka he try to remove the kailayam pl.

forgive my lord for this blind mistakes. Siva had offered him **Atma linga** on one condition basis. i.e **He should not keep this lingam in the floor** on the way while proceeding to srilanka upon reaching lanka ask him to install it there and make a regular prayer to this linga you will not get defeated by any one.

The Saint Narada conveyed this enriched power will be attained by Ravana when he install the Atma lingam in lanka. In order to avoid this is to happen INDIRAN seeks VISHNU help and the VISHNU gave an idea to VARUNA to make Ravana feel thrust and fill his stomach with water due to this Ravana felt urine. Ravana was desperate to releieve himself. The Ravana tried manyways not to keep linga in the floor Seeing Lord Ganesha in the form of a brahmin boy, he gave it to him to hold, By the time he returun back the lingam has been kept in place called **Sitapoomela** present day Vaidyanath temple premises in Deogarh. On his return Ravana found the lingam in the floor he try to remove since it is Jothirlingam not able to shack by Ravana finaly he left the lingam there and went to Lanka. After several years back while his return to india he found this lingam has been maitained by Pijunath(hunter) on his request he made one well called chandirakoop you can find this now also and built the temple too named after this hunter name.

Some of the purans describe the advent of Baidyanath of Deoghar to the 'Satya Yug', or the first age of the world. When Sakti, the wife of lord SHIVA and the daughter of DAKSHA RAJA committed suicide in consequence of the discourtesy shown to her husband by Raja Daksha, after SHE died the body has been took by Siva and made Korathandavam during that time the Sakti's body part fallen several place across the india, Where the famous sakti Peedams were installed across india. Where the heart falling spot of Deoghar (Baidyanath) of SHIVA'S Sati attends is sanctity. Hence the place had been called as 'SIDDHAPEETH'

PUNIYA THEERTHAM

Chandirakoop well. In the north of the temple there is one holy pond known as 'SIVGANGA', regarding which there are several myths in the society. Its present condition is brought by king of Laxmipur state (Late Thakur Pratap Narayan Dev). Adjacent to it there is another old pond (Mansinghi) made during 16th century by Swami Raja Man Singh (Jaipur).

CEREMONY /POOJA

In the sharavan month (June to August months) people bring ganga Kavadi from 130Km distance to this temple for Iswar Abisekam purpose. During this period the Lord Siva had poison and kept it in his throat due to that his body become warm to cool HIM the linga has been washed with ganga water latter on with vilva tree leaves it is covered. It is believed it cools HIS body i.e lacks of people took holy kavadi during this period. The devotee chant with Mantra of **Bum bum—Boolo, Bum bum—Boola** all the way during the Ganga kavadi procession. Morning time the Baba was washed with Chandrakup theerth water offered by devotees. In the evening the linga was initially washed with water than Decorated nicely with flower like cone shape you cannot find main lingam that time, it has been covered with flowers decoration as mentioned above.

TEMPLE ADMINISTRATION

Though it's original citizens are Panari and Adams, now several religious persons are residing. But priest group of 'Maithil Brahmins came here in the end of 13th century and beginning of 14th century from Mithila Kingdom known as Darbhanga. Radhi Brahmins came here from Bengal, Kanyakubja also came from Central India during during 16th century. These all priest groups assist Shivas worshipper by giving shelter and other help. Their regardless contribution can be seen in maintaining the sanctity of the temple.

During my visit to the temple i had seen Sringar darshan we are allow to touch lingam. The administration activities such as is controlled by the head priest his post is known as 'Sevayat' who is not only head priest but religious administrator too. Worshippers can approach to him he will receive the devotees co-ordially. Presently the administration of the temple is under one Trust whose members are from local pandit community representative of king Giddhor and Deputy Commissioner Deoghar being receiver.

The king of Giddhor donates the lot of heavy gold vessels to temple and in other way several freedom fighter Vinoba Bhave, Mahatma Gandhi, B. N. Jha and Ram Raj Jajware tries their best to open the temple gate for other sectors of people. Inspite of having such a large contradiction, the people here remain unity and continue their life with total freedom. During sharavan months lacks of people gather at temple to offer sacred Ganaga water to lord Siva, which has been brought approx 130 Km away from the temple. The devotees brings this water all the by trekking and offer this sacred water lord siva in Baithiyanath temple.

OTHER PLACES TO SEE NEAR BY

The Statue of Ravana with his 10 head. It is revealed in our scared books Ravana carried out tabus in this place and got Atma lingam from lord Siva. Other temple nearby to see from jothir lingam distance were mentioned. 1. Naw lacka temple (Bhagavan-Gopalji)-2Km 2. Nava durga temple (1Km) 3. Balananda Ashram (2Km). 4. Basukinath Mandir (35 Km) 5. Sri Sir Mohan temple (2Km) 6. Nandan hill (4Km) 7. Trikut parvatham 8. Tapovan 9. AnKul thakur Satsang (Ramakrishna mission) 10. Satsang nagar 11. Paagal baba Ashram 12. Sultan ganj (135Km) from where the Ganga jel brought to Baidyanath for Abishekam purpose.

Nau lacka temple:

This temple is made with good architect and Gopalji (Krishnan) shrine is there the Guru Balananda Bramachari statue is there. In Balananda Ashram the Guru Statue kept in the Marble made shrine with Good architect of north Indian style. In the balanada ashram Siva shrine and Bhagavathi shrines are there. You can relax under the beneath of the isthala viruchum tree inside the ashram.

Nava Durga temple.

In this temple at evening 6:30 Pm the Maa Aarthi is carried out for half an hour it is good to see. In this temple for Lord Shiva with Parvathi in Staute form murthi available, it is rare to see and Lord Krishna shrine also there. The Durga's various leela painted nicely in wall painting. This temple is maintain by Dev Sang it also runs Dev Sang school for local people education purpose.

Ankul Thakur Sat Sang (Ramakrishna mission)

In this Sat sang at evening 7 o clock Sat sang is good have a time to participate in this sat sang.

Nandan Hill park:

Here the park is maintained well for children's to refresh and play jula and various playing arrangement is there spent some time with your family here.

Basukinath temple.

The temple is 35km from Deogarh it is also having Siva Ganga pond the temple looks similar to Deogarh temple but size is smaller than Jothir lingam shrine.

END OF CHAPTER 2.2

Chapter 2.3

KEDARNATH TEMPLE

This shrine is located in himaliya at height of 11,735 feet above sea level, where the shrine is known by several names such as Gandhamadana parvatham, Sumera parvatham, Pancha parvatham, etc. Pancha parvatham means the five mountain sacred peaks closely located namely Rudra Himalayas, Vishnupuri, Brahmapuri, Udayagiri & Swargarohini. Kedarnath located at the head of the Mandakini River, is amongst the holiest pilgrimages for Hindu devotees. The temple, believed to be very ancient, and has been continousally renovated over the period. According to myth, Lord Shiva wished to evade from the Pandavas, and took refuge in Kedarnath in the form of a bull. On being followed, He dived into the ground, leaving behind His hump of the surface. The hump is worshipped in the temple of Kedarnath unlike its usual form it is pyramidal and considered as one of the 12 Jyotirlings. The remaining parts of the body are worshipped at four other places the **arms (Bahu) at Tungnath, the face (mukh) at Rudranath, the navel (nabhi) at Madmaheshwar and hair (jata) at Kalpeshwar.**

Together with Kedarnath, these places are known as the Pancha Kedar. The sannadhi of the Lord is facing south. There are the idols of Kedaragowri, Krishna, Pandavas, Draupadi, Vinayagar, Veerabadrar, Kaarthikeyan, and Nandi. The shrine is covered by snow for 6 months in a year. It is believed during this time the Devas are worshipping the Lord.

It is considered to be visiting kedernath along with Pashupatinath in Nepal would complete the pilgrimage. Lord Shiva assumed the form of wild boar and dived into the earth at Kedarnath and emerges at Pashupatinath. Kedarnath forms a part of the smaller Char Dham pilgrimage circuit of Hindus. It is also one of the Padal Petra isthalam of Norht India mentioned in Thevaaram rymes. Pure ghee is offered at Kedarnath lingam as the boar was injured.

At the approach of winters in the month of November, the holy statue of Lord Shiva, is carried down from Kedarkhand to Ukhimath, and is reinstating at Kedarnath, in the first week of May every year. It is the time that the doors of the temple are open to pilgrims, who come from all parts of India, for a holy pilgrimage. The shrine of Kedarnath is placed in such a place and is surrounded by lofty, snow covered mountains, and grassy meadows in all the valleys. Immediately behind the temple, is the high Keadar dome peak, which can be sighted from far away? The sight of the temple and the peak with its long-lasting snows is, simply, an enchanting sight.

TEMPLE BUILT

The ancient temple was built by Pandavas around 3030 BC in Pancha Parvatham or sumeru Parvatham hills in Himalaya at an altitude of 3586 meter high. Latter on it was renovated by Adisankarar.

JOURNEY TO THE TEMPLE

From Delhi by train or bus reach haridwar, from haridwar to Gowrikunt 260Km by road, either by bus or hired vechile. From Gowrikunt the tough trekking start you have to prepare for that by taking sufficient rest in any of these villages namely Nalashety,

Rampur, Paydushety and Bettashety. From Gowrikunt to Kedernath temple 14 km, for going this Dolly and horse facility too available. Prior to start any mode of journey take bath in the hot water pond called Thapthakunt then strat your journey. Haridwar-Rishikesh() __ Rishikesh –Devaprayagai(70Km), here the river Paakerati and Alagananda rivers join together, __Devaprayagai-Ruthraprayagai(34km) here Mandakani river jons to Alagananda river __ Ruthraprayagai-Agasthiyar saint village(13Km)__ Agasthiyar saint village-Gupta kasi(21Km), the Gupta kasi to Rampur, The Rampur to Triyuginarayan where Parvathi and lord siva marriage happened.

From May month beginning to October month end the temple kept open for devotees, avoid the journey during rainy season from 3rd week of July to second week of September. During winter season the temple kept closed no one available here.

ISTHALAM HISTORY

Mythology states that the deity of Kedarnath temple is identified with the rump of a bull. The Mahabharat war even though made victory to Pandavas and ruled under Dharma leadership for 36 years, they were deeply suffered by war effect, during war the close relatives to them were killed and thousands of peoples were died. Hence the Dharma Monarched the Arjun's grand son Parisit as a king and all the Pandavas with thropathy left for Vanasprastham yatra towards Kasi temple but they could not able to see Lord Siva there, as the lord depart to the Himalaya hills during that period. The Pandavas also proceed to the Himalaya to find Lord Siva and get his bless and to purify their sin caused due to war. Since it was not time designated for humans to worship the Lord here, Lord Siva tried to go away in the form of a bull.

Goddess Gowri

Gourikund-An ancient temple dedicated to the Goddess GOWRI or Parvati, the Gowrikund houses the metallic idols of Gowri and Shiva. According to legend, Parvati meditated here for a long time, to win Shiva as HER consort. Ultimately, she succeeded, and the cosmic couple was wed at Thriuginarayan.

One day they were relaxing in hills land slide the Bhima found one Bullack in a crowd of cows behaves differently, the Bhima try to catch this bullack but it escaped from him and rushed into Soil heap there and got trapped. As the half of the front portion of bullack inside the soil heap and another half left out back portion was outside, the Bhima try to pull out this bullack from soil heap he failed in his effort. The bullock become strong rock during this course of time, bhima try to break this rock with his Gada, whilst a loud voice heard that warns Bhima to stop his activity, the stunned Bhima stand like a statue and watched astonishingly with his brothers. From this rock the Lord Siva come out and showed his VISWARUPAM to all pandavas. The Pandavas chant with mantra and prayed HIM several ways and requested lord Siva to nullify their war Sins. The Lord accepted their request and created Ganga theertham there, and ask them to take holy bath in that theertham. Again lord siva infuse into that rock and become Jothirling there, in this place present Kedernath temple exisit. The Pandavas first built the temple and made pooja to Lord Siva here. Latter on the pandavas made Mahaprasthana yatra from here. Here the Nar Narayan (Vishnu avatar) made penance in badhri ashram to please HIM, Lord Siva appered and Express TATHA ISTHU after Narayan had darshan HE disappears.

SCULPTURE WORK

The entrance starts with the statue of Nandi, the divine bull of Shiva. Fine & detailed carvings exhibiting images can be seen on the walls inside. The exterior of the temple is rather simple, but the interior is adorned with marvellous sculptures. In the Garbagirah is an irregular shaped conical rock which is about five feet by four feet.

PUNIYA THIRTHAM

Ganga river, Mandakini river, Devaprayagai, Ruthraprayagai and Gowrikunt.

OTHER PLACES TO SEE NEAR BY

In Rishikesh Sivanandar ashram, laksman jula hanging bridge, Badrinath, Agni kunt in Triyugi narayan temple. Vasuki Tal Situated at an altitude of 14, 200 ft, and 6 kms away from Kedarnath, Vasuki Tal is situated on the right side of the valley. Son Prayag located at the confluence of the Mandakini and the Sone-Ganga, this quaint village is known for its picturesque beauty. Mandakini River Ghat where devotees takes holy bath on the way to kedernath.

END OF CHAPTER 2.3

Chapter 2.4

OMKARESHWAR TEMPLE

**OM AERIAL VIEW
OF ISLAND
TOOK FROM FLIGHT**

MAIN TEMPLE VIEW

OLD BRIDGE CONNECTING MAIN LAND AND TEMPLE

MAIN TEMPLE OVERVIEW

AMALESHWAR TEMPLE LOCATED IN MAIN LAND IN OMKARESHWAR

Just next to the white structure you can see a recently constructed portion where people sitting in the picture behind of me, it helps you go from level two to level three, where you can approach to Omkareshar, next Mahakaleshwar. at each level is a mandir ie, Siddheshwar & Manshadevi, Gupteshwar and Dhwajeshwar that are on three levels. Since Level three to five is within the structure itself its Internal staircases are quite difficult to climb only one person can claim at a time I had reached upto the top of the temple where you can find top hole visible in white structure you can approach upto this floor by internal staircase.

The Omkareshawar temple is built in the North Inidan style of architecture, with high spires. Devotees consider worship to Panchamuga Ganesha, to be very auspicious. There is a shrine for Annapoorani. Siva Lingas of various sizes are sold in great numbers in this place. Omkareshwar is situated on the Mandhata hills in Madhya Pradesh, known in ancient times as Shivpuri. The temple dates back to the Krita Yuga.

Omkareshwar, the sacred island, shaped like the holiest of all Hindu symbols, `Om`, has drawn to it hundreds of generations of pilgrims. Here, at the confluence of the rivers Narmada and Kaveri, the devotee gather to kneel before the Jyotirlinga (one of the twelve throughout India) at the temple of Shri Omkar Mandhata. Left picture An overview of Omkareshwar Jyotirling ie on the banks of the river Narmadaji. What you see in front is the Narmada river, at the base is a ghat, the Nagar community has recently constructed this very beautiful and clean ghat where devotees bath in the Narmada.

The aerial view shows On The island comprises two lofty hills and is divided by a valley in such a way that it appears in the shape of the sacred Hindu symbol `Om` from above. Between the precipitous hills of the Vindhya on the North and the Satpura on the South, the Narmada forms a deep silent pool which in former times was full of alligators and fish, so tame as to take grain from human hand.

TEMPLE BUILT

The samrat Mandhata born in Ishwago generation directly from his father Yuvanachsavan before to Lord Rama birth in this land, ruled this region its capital was Ayodiya. He dfeated Ravana, forgived and left him alive. The Mandhata made reqular worship and pooja to this lingam and stayed in this place most of his period, hence this place has been called in his name. It is believed the temple might have been built by **Gupta kings in 4 to 5th century**. It has got small lingam around which the water comes naturally even though its elevation higher than many feet from Narmada river water level. A closer view the Omkareshwar Jyotirling temple it has five levels.

SCUPLTURE WORK IN THE TEMPLE

The temple stands on a one-mile long, half-mile wide island formed by the fork of the Narmada. The soft stone of which it was constructed has lent its pliable surface to a rare degree of detailed work, of which the frieze figures on the upper portion are the most striking. Also intricately carved is the stone roof of the temple. Encircling the shrine are verandahs with columns which are carved in circles, polygons and squares. The saba hall pillars having some sculpture work and the temple is situated on a hillock.

JOURNEY TO THE TEMPLE.

The temple is located in omkareshwar in Madhya Pradesh where **River Narmada And River Kaveri Meet**; from Indore only 75km by road we can reach this temple. For Indore flight and train service avialble from main cities. From Khanduva Road railway station 77Km to omkareshwar most of the pilgrims utilize the train facility. From southern bank of Narmada River the cantilever bridge connecting the main land and this island. The new bridge constructed during the last Simhastha held in 2004 you can cross the river Narmada on to Omkareshwar in various ways. You can take the new or old bridge or take a boat ride. A view of the new bridge. As you see it is supported by columns on either side of the river. Nearest airport is Indore Ahilyabai airport. The temple is located in between Indore and Khanduwa main road almost equal distance from either from Indore or Khanduwa. The nearest railway station is Omkareshwar road small railway station. From this station 14km by road we have to travel for this Minivan facility available an average of every half an hour. In muttuwa the Narmada river over bridge is constructed all the vehicle pass through this bridge only. From indore also the Minibus operates direcly to Omkareshwar temple.

From Indore most of the travel is along the forest area only. You can find Narmada River crossing at hill lock in many places. A drinking water pipe taken from Narmada River leads to Indore you can find along the road side in the forest area. Almost 40 km the train or buses pass through this forest route. From Indore almost 30 Km distance you can find Shanni Mandir in Paigan near simrol on main road, you can visit this temple.

The early morning visit to OMKARESHWAR temple makes more pleasure in our mind the temple is located in island in the shape of Sacred Hindu symbol OM. The check dam built in the river across and river passes through deep valley and Nagar community built Ghats is there. The devotees takes bath in Narmada river and visit to Amaleshwar than proceed to Omkareshwar temple through the hanging bridge built across the Narmada River. In this temple tower only the devotees allowed to visit the other floor in the towers. For this purpose a small steps leads to each floor only one person only can claim at a time a narrow passage.

In the Narmada River boat takes along the river you can have this marvellous journey and have your sweet memories of Omkareshwar in your life term. For visiting this temple especially one day required start early morning from Indore the local buses takes almost 2.5 to 3 hrs to reach the temple. It is better to depart before 6 o' clock in the evening and return to Indore after wards the vehicles facility not available much from Omkareshwar.

The Banalingam is very famous here you can collect the same and make pooja in the house using this. In Narmada River naturally formed more Banalingam available. From thadikunt especially you can find more varieties of Banalingam. From Indore only 65KM for Ujjain here you can find Mahakal Jothirlingam and various historic event things of olden days you can find till now, this olden footprints were preserved and kept for public visit don't miss it during your visit.

ISTHALAM HISTORY

As tempted by the **saint Naratha**, The vindhya hills would like to grow Greater than Mahameru parvatha hills, in this regard as per Naratha advice the Vindiyan made penance towards lord Siva. He draws an OMKARA shape yantiram in that he installed the lingam made up of soil and made continuous pooja for six months. By seeing his worship lord Siva appeared in front of him and offered boon as per his desire to Grow but on one condition basis, it should not make disturbance to others. If disturbance caused any complaints arises you will be advised and controlled by one of my Rishis. But the Vindhyas did not stop growing, and even obstructed the sun and the moon. Sage Agasthyar subdued its growth by saying it should not grow till he gets back from south to there. He never went back & hence the growth was arrested. The Lord Siva manifest himself as OMKARA shape hill in Narmada River in this place, the Vindiyan worshiped Lingam become Jothirlingam in this island. The other legend there Was A War Between Devils Who And The Lords In Which Devils Got Victory Over The Lord. Thus the Devil started There Misdeeds On Earth. At This Lord Shiva Came to Earth in the Form of Omkareshwar to Give Strength to All the Lords to Fight with the Devils. Lord Brahma and Lord Vishnu Are Believed to Be Here.

It is believed the devatos are making worship from sky now also, you can here there mantra chanting voice when you claim to this hill top and stand towards east direction try during your visit.

Omkareshwar Temple the Jyotir Lingam split into two, and there are two Siva lingams, Omkareswarar & Amaleshwarar (Amareshwarar).

PUNIYA THIRTHAM

Narmada River in Omkareshwar and Thaiadikunt theertham.

CEREMONY

The Sivratri and karthikay month fullmoon day festivals were famous here.

OTHER PLACES TO SEE NEAR BY

Gowri somnath temple lingam, without roof presently available sitanath temple, Maleshwar temple, Rinmuktheswarar, Kedareshwarar, the suicide rock in this hills and in the river bank you can find Annapurna Ashiram, Markendaya Ashiram and sarvana Ashiram. The caves of **Guru Govind bhagavat paathar** who is **Guru to Adisankarar** made Tabus in this place. The cave his recently found in 1978 by Jabulpur Nagaraj Sharma, the Bhopal Kanchi Kama Kodi Pedam made renovation work and Sri Jayanthira saraswathi swamiji made inaguration to this caves in 21st Apl-1987 and allowed for public seeing. Vikramathithyan (son of Guru govind) Statue. Thadikunt where we can get The Special lingam called Banaalingam which is used for Panchaaedana pooja purpose located 25Km from this palce by boat we can reach to this place.

END OF CHAPTER 2.4

Chapter 2.5

MAHAKAL TEMPLE

God Name-Mahakaleshwar. HIS linga height is 2 ft.

The temple here is situated beside the cremation grounds and it is said that the ashes of this cremation ground is taken for puja in the temple in olden days. According to the legend Shiva vanquished the demon Dushana here. The glory of the Mahakaleshwar Temple has been mentioned in the Tamil hymns of the Nayanmar saints of the 1st millenium CE.

The Mahakaleshwar temple is made in five levels, one of which is underground. The Temple is surrounded by huge walls. The Temple peak is decorated with fine sculptures. The underground sanctum is lightened by brass lamps. The idol of Omkareshwar Shiva is consecrated in the sanctum above the Mahakal shrine. The idol in the temple is known as Dakshinamurti, facing the south direction in Garbagirah. The shree yantra perched upside down at the ceiling of the Garbagirah (where the Shiv Lingam sits). The idols in the temple are all strategically placed like the images of Ganesh, Parvati and Karttikeya installed in the west, north and east direction respectively. The image of Nandi is situated in the south direction. The idol of Nagchandreshwar is situated in the third storey and pilgrims are allowed to pay homage to the diety only on the day of Nagapanchami. Among the 12 Jyotirlingas, the Mahakal Jyotirlinga is believed to be swayambhu, meaning 'born of itself'. It is believed that the holy powers of the Jyotirlinga are self derived from within and unlike other Jyotirlinga; they are not ritually established through Mantra Shakti. The prasada in the temple can be re-offered unlike other temples. This temple has many shrines in its Pragaram they are Narasimar, Mangala nathar, Sidha nathar, Sintha Harna Ganapathi, Vital pandari nathar, Pragaspathasvar Mahadevan, Swapneshwar Mahadevan, Snakatmotcha sitha Hanuman, Visthabhaswarar Mahadevan, Hanuman, Sakshi Gopal, Sidi Ganesha, Vada virutcham, Egathasa lingeshwarar, Navagrahas, Neelakandeshwarar, Kaanthaveshwarar, Govindeshwarar Mahadevan, Anathi Kalbeshwarar, Suaptha risihigal, Omkareshwarar, Managameshwarar, Rameshwarar& Viswanathar. In this temple the Navagraghas and Sauptharishigal were shown in linga forms. The idol of the Mahakaleshwar is Dhakshinamurti, located at the NAVAL point of the earth facing the south. The only jyothirlinga of its kind. This fact has a special significance in the TANTRIC tradition. The idol of the Omkareshwar is consecrated in the sanctum above the Mahakaleshwar shrine(First floor in the picture. The idol of Nagchandreshwar on the third floor(just below the shikhara) is open for Darshan only on the day of Nagpanchmi. The Mahasivaratri celebration is very famous here.

HARSIDHI AMMAN

**MAHAKALESHWAR
TEMPLE FRONT VIEW**

**BADA GANAPATHY
TEMPLE**

GADHAKALIKA TEMPLE

YANTAR MANDIR SHOWS SHADOW TIME

RAM GHAT IN SIPRA RIVER

TEMPLE BUILT

The ancient temple renovated in 11th century and it was destroyed completely by **Delhi Sultan illtutmish in 1234 CE**. He taken all the valuables inside the temple and removed the Mahakaleshwar jothirlingam from its Garbagirah and thrown into the Kodi thirtham. On old temple top he built the **Kaliyabeer**. About 500 years no one paid attention to this jothirlingam. In **18th century** the Marata commandant Ranonis captured india and started ruling this place as per his order the Diwan Ramachandira Rao senvi find out the Jothirlingam from the ruined Kodi pond. After proper pooja he installed back the Jotirling in its old place and new temple built there. The stone structure of ground, first and second floors seems to be 18th century, while the temple Shikhar looks like modern construction. During last Simhastha things were improved further.

JOURNEY TO THE TEMPLE

Delhi to Bhopal by train, from Bhopal 180 Km to Ujjain.

SCUPLTURE WORK IN THE TEMPLE

The temple has been located near Rudhra sakar Lake. It main entrance is from East. It had many Kalasamand largest one had height of 88ft. Sikaraha.

ISTHALAM HISTORY

In holy Shipra river bank the town called Avanthipuri was there. The Vedapriyan with his four sons Devapriyan, Medan, Suvidaran, Dharumavathi were lived here. They were cary out prayer to Lord Siva dedicately over day and night for many years sincerely with strong devotion. Near by Avanthipuri the demon called Dusanan ruled arogantly and tortured all people who ever involved in ritual worhship. One day the Dusanan with his soldiers attack the Avanthipuri town and ask all of them to surrender to him and stop their ritual worship immediately. The shocked local people rushed to Vedapriyan son's houses told their problem. The elder son of him Devapriyan told to all of this locals nothing to worry ask them to continue their worship towards Lord Siva HE will take care everything. The Dusanan upon hearing this message came to Devapriyan house and ask them stop immediately all ritual worship but they neglect his words and continue the pooja conciously. The anoyed Dusanan order his soldire to kill them. The spot where they had taken mud to make the Lingam, had become a huge pond. When Dushanan came to disturb their pooja, from this pond the Agni form (magma) came out from that one Lingam formed. This Lingam broken into two from that the Lord Siva came with long hair and tiger skin worn around his body and look at the demon (Raksas) with loud huming and very anguishly by seeing HIM all the demons become ash. On the request of the Brahmins and local people Lord Siva settle back in that lingam gave darshan to Devotees at this isthalam as Mahakaleshwarar in present Ujjain temple. After visiting varagha mandir took bath in Sipra River than visit the Mahakall temple. Ram Ghat where the Simhastha (known as Kumbh in Prayag) is held.

PUNIYA THEERTHAM

The KODI thirtham inside the temple it has got four well inside from these different colors of fresh water make up this theertham. Narasing Ghat, Ram Ghat, chathri ghat and Ganga ghat is avialble in sipra river banks for taking holy bath. Apart from this Mohana theertham and kandarva theertham too available.

SPECIAL DECORATION OF LINGA

In auspicious days the linga has been Decorated in many forms, in that **MEVA (Bhasm) decoration** you should see. For this MEVA decoration they utilize the dry fruits like graphs, nuts, dals for making face of the God. The lingam has been decorated like head with flowers, eyes, nose, mostatch what you see is Bhasm Shringar.

The Ghee light glows 24 Hrs inside Garbagirah, the **EARLY Morning POOJA called PANCHUBASARAM** for this Abisaygam, the ash brought from Graveyard is used latter on it has distributed to all devotees as Prasad. The Bhasm aarti starts every morning at about 4am and complete by 6am approx. Stand in the line 2hrs before to this time, than you can able to sit close to Garbagirah and watch the bhasm or ashes are offered to the lingam. The chanting of mantras during aarti creates good vibration around us you can experience the same when you present there In November month as per North indian calander Krishnabhaksa sadurtasi day (Diwali day) with the BUNK(ABIN) ring like form(kaaupu) made on linga and kept upto 10am, latter on it has been washed with warm water.

CERMONY

In ujjain 12 years once Kumbamela carried out during that time you can find lot of sadus in this place for one month period. The Mahasivaratri and Karthiga month (December) fullmoon day festival carried out remarkably.

OTHER PLACES TO SEE NEAR BY

It has got other 84 siva temple,36 goddess temple,12 vishnu 8 Biravr temple, 11 Rudhra temples and 6 Ganesha temples. **Shanthipani ashram** where lord krishna, balarama and kusaylar learnt veda from saint Shanthipani and its near by Purusotham sagar and Solasagar lakes, Gopal mandir in chathri chouk, Harasid amman temple, Gadha kali mandir and its near by sidhavadam, Paruthrahari caves, Badaa ganapathi, Panchamuga Hanuman, and Mangalnath temple sevai gragham. Yantiramahal.

HARASIDHI AMMAN TEMPLE:

It is believed that the Goddess of this temple Mataji remains at Koila Dungar temple in Porbander for twelve hours and comes to Ujjain ka temple in the evening during aarti time. A view of Harasidhi Amman mandir. The king Vikramaditya favourite temple he made regular pooja here.

GADHAKALIKA MANDIR:

Shri Gadhkalika mandir is traditionally known to be the choice of worship of the greatest poet Kalidasa – the author of Abigyna Shakuntala and chief gem of the court of Raja Vikramaditya. Images and bricks & part of the plinth are of the 1st century B.C. (Shunga period), 4th century A.D. (Gupta period) and 10th century A.D. (Parmar period) were recovered from the basement of the temple. Emperor Harshvardhan renovated this temple in the 7th century a.d. – there is some indication of its further renovation in the 10th century a.d. under Parma rule. Right side picture is sancturm and left side picture is Full view of Gadhkali Mandir.

24 KAMBA MATA KA MANDIR:

24 Khamba Mata ka Mandir. What you can see in the present days is the old entrance of the Mahakaleshwarar Temple. Where the ancient temple consists of huge complex there the houses come up today.

MANGALNATH MANDIR:

According to Matsya puran, this is the birth place of Mangalgraha or Mars. Flowing Shipra river presents a very beautiful view in front of the temple. Devotees gather in large numbers especially on Tuesday. Located on a hillock, this place represents the highest place in the area. In ancient times, the place was famous as it is said to have provided a clear view of

Mars – Ujjain was an important center for astronomical. studies. This place, traditionally known for its suitability for astronomical readings of mars continues to hold its religious importance.

UJJAIN HISTORY:

Ujjain comes from Ujjainee, which means one who conquers with pride. It is situated on the banks of the river Shipra. Enjoyed a position of considerable importance in the field of astronomy. Great works on astronomy such as the Surya Siddhanta and the Panch Siddhanta were written in Ujjain. According to Indian astronomers, the Tropic of Cancer is supposed to pass through Ujjain. It is also the fist meridian of longitude of the Hindu geographers. From about the 4th century BC, Ujjain enjoyed the reputation of being India's Greenwich. The observatory today was built by Raja Jai Singh (1686-1743), who was a great scholar. Ujjain his famous for space science and astrology of those days here one research centre Yantiramahal reveals that one. Maruchakadigam, Kadampari, Kadasarithra sagar, Sivalela amrutham, Megasanthesam like books reveals about Ujjain history you can go through this books for details.

The famous kings Vikramathithiyan, Salivahanan, Ashok samrat son Mahindra varman and his daughter Sangamithra born in Ujjain. The famous poets like Kalidasan, Thanvanthri, kashnabagar, Amarasimar, Sangu, Vedalapattar, Kadagarparar, Varhamigurar, Thandi, Pavapoothi, Paruthrahari and vararusi lived in this place during Vikramaditya period.

The other names for Ujjain: Ujjaini, Avanti, Pratikalpa, Vishala, Kumudhati, Kushsthali, Chudamani, Kanak Srange, Padmavati.

END OF CHAPTER 2.5

Chapter 2.6

NAGAESHWAR TEMPLE

The lingam is facing South, with the Gomugam facing East. There is a story for this position. A devotee by name Naamdev was singing bhajans in front of the Lord. Other devotees asked him to stand aside and not hide the Lord. To this Naamdev asked them to suggest one direction in which the Lord does not exist, so that he can stand there. The enraged devotees carried him and left him on the southside. To their astonishment, they found that the Linga was now facing South with the Gomugam facing East. The temple has got 85ft High Lord Siva statue this may be largest in size in its kind. In this temple for shanni separate statue is there beneath of the tree. The temple near by one park which houses Lord Siva, Parvathi, Ganesha and Muruga together sitting on hill top like Status made nice to see.

TEMPLE BUILT

The ancient temple totally damaged condition in this place new temple constructed.

SCUPLTURE WORK IN THE TEMPLE.

Except Gigantic 85 ft high JADATHARAN statue nothing available.

JOURNEY TO THE TEMPLE

From any Metro cities in India, train/flight facility available for Ahemadabad. From ahemadabad catch trains to Okha via Rajkot and alight at Okha. From Okha 20 km by bus, on the way towards Pet Dwaraga town. Now days for Rajkot also you can go by flight. From Rajkot to duwaraka or Okha by train 240Km it tooks 3.5hrs. From Duwaraka 22 km to Nageshwar Jothir lingam.

ISTHALAM HISTORY

The saints were lived in the THARUKAVANAM had occupied with more Ego and thinking that they were not lesser than any god and not carried ritual worship to Gods. In other hand the saints wives due to their pathini(trueness to their husband) upkeeping caused for such a high status in the society. They paved a way to unethical life styles to realize them truth of Dharma the Siva came as a Manmadan(A man looking very handsome) to flatter wives of all saints. The vishnu came as a beautiful women to flatter all saints. Both of them were succed in their goals at one stage all wives of saints were glamorly dressed following Lord siva madly, at the same time the saints were following glamor vishnu called as Mohini in opposite side. The all the saints from far seen their wifes bad condition they run back from that spot and had a group discussion among them about how to overcome from this trickly trapped Situation. They had got more angry on both of them try to find their motive behind. The saints called upon them try to negotiate but it become more argument, they cursed them in several ways without knowing who they are what for they came. Since their curse not affected them in any way finally they decided to vanish them with TANTRA technique that also end up in failure. The saints returned to their house due to their inability and lord Ishwar made different kind of THANDAVAM(the dance made by lord siva) infront of Vishnu. After lord vishnu departure from their the Iswar took a shelter in snakes burrow.

The very next day onwards the Tharukavanam saints affected by unknown desease, over the period they become very weak. They requested Brama to help them to come out from this desease, the brama had explained entire sceneria (Iswar lila) to the saints to realize their mistakes. Upon brama verdict they came to snake burrow where Iswar taken shelter and made regular poojas and worship in that place. The Iswar admired by their ritual pratice and gave Darsan to them in Agni Form, from this Agni the Jothirlingam came out. The five head King cobra engulf this lingam in its base and stand behind of it like crown to the Lingam, The Naga(Naga means one type of cobra snake) lingam exists in this form here, hence the temple called as Nageshwar (Naga +Iswar=Nageshwar). The weapons, animals and etc were used against maheswar was worn by HIM as a ornament and costumes, descriping this posture The biggest STATUE with Gijantic size with 82 ft high present in this temple. Once uopn a time, the Tharugan and his wife thrugai lead a life in Tharukavanam. They were heading Sea pyrates group, in olden days whatever ships came to this Okha port has been attacked by this gang. Hence in their name this place has been called as THARUKAVANAM.

The other history behind this temple is A Siva devotee, Supriya who was a merchant reached the Darukavanam, where Daruka lived with his wife Daruki, while sailing with his goods. Daruka asked Supriya to teach him the path of devotion to Siva, the norms of performing pooja and penance. Fearing that Daruka would use any additional powers gained by such penance, to bad use,

NAGESHWAR JOTHIRLINGAM TEMPLE OVER VIEW

DUWARAKA KRISHNA TEMPLE

SWAMY NARAYANA TEMPLE IN JAMNAGAR

Supriya refused to guide him. The enraged Daruka began to torture Supriya. Supriya however was staunch in her faith in the Lord and was unmoved by any torture. Lord Siva was pleased and appeared and killed the demon Daruka. Daruki, Daruka's wife, now started giving even more trouble than her husband. Siva vanquished her too and gives darshan to his devotees at this place as Nageshwar. During **Duwabra yugam Lord Krishna** had made big township in this place i.e present Duwaraga town.

PUNIYA THERTHAM: Nil.

CEREMONY

In Tamil one proverb is there. i.e. Pathinarum petru Peru valzyu kanga (meaning is have a sixteen kind of things to lead a successful life). They are family life, good health, handsome physic, stronger body, Pleasure, knowledge, good attitude, excellence, blessed child, happiness, wealth, Ruling power, long life, Charming, Atma puification and Ulitimate of life callled Mukthi. To get all these you can visit this temple, because his face in JADATHARAN statue so calm, like a massive view of siva you cannot find any where. By seeing HIM you will be blessed with this all.

OTHER PLACES TO SEE

Duwaraka Krishna Temples:

The Duwaraka was established and ruled by Lord Krishna. During ruling time he use to stay in duwaraka and to take rest, he use to stay in Pet Duwaraka island.

The Krishna temple is located in the River bed Komoki where it joins with Arabic sea. From here the city trip bus is available that takes us to all the temples located in and around Duwaraka.

During your visit you must **visit Main temple first, Nageshwar jothir lingam, Gopi talab, Pet duwaraka Krishna mandir where you can find 5500 years old Rukmani installed Duwarakinath moorthi** in the temple. For reaching this temple we have to travel by boat from OKHA to Pet Duwaraka. In Pet Duwaraka 5000 muslims and 2000 Hindus were there. Here the Krishnas's younger age friend SUDHAMA who lived in Porbander, met Krishna and offered some rice to Krishna. Hence whoever Devotees goes to Pet duwaraka considered as SUDHMA, in the name of Sudama people offer rice donation to the temple Administrater. It will be distributed to Brahmins lives in this island. At the end the Devotees visit Rukmani mandir in Duwaraka entrance with this the Duwaraka Pilgrimage completes.

RUKMANI MANDIR.

In India for Rukmani two places worship type temples are there. One in Maharastra and other in Duwaraka. Whoever goes to this temple has to drink the water offered by temple administrator. There is a history behind that. When Rukmani filled with self proud about her family, Krishna would like to taught her effectiveness of leading simple lifestyle. In this regard He adviced her to invite Durvasa Rishi to Duwaraka. The Rishi accepted rukmani request on one condition if Both Krishna and Rukmani pull his charot all the way to Duwaraka he would like to come to there. The rukmani accepted Rishi's conditional visit to duwaraka and pull the charot of him, while on the way she felt more thrusty and requested Krishna to provide her some water. The lord Krishna made a well were the Ganga water tend to flow as per Krishna request. In this course they forget to host Durvasa Rishi and the Rishi question their courtesy and felt angry and cursed both of them has to leave separate for 12 years and in Duwaraka region they will not get any pure water, the water will become salty. The people of Duwaraka still believe this truth as the all ground water in and around here is still salty except this Krishna made well.

This holy water you will get it don't miss it to drink during your visit.

Due to the Rishi curse Rukmani to stay separate Krishna built this temple for Rukmani.

GOPI THALAB:

Where Lord Krishna rescued lot of gopies along with arjuna when they were taken into custody by thiefs while they take bath in Gopi thalab. Here you can find Radha and Lakshmi narayana temples. Here from the pond the soil taken out was made us soil stick which is used for applying Nama.

END OF CHAPTER 2.6

Chapter 2.7

SOMNATH TEMPLE

Godname-Somanath, Godessname-Gowrimatha. It is believed that the Moon (Chandra) worshipped lord Siva at Somanth Temple to get rid of King Daksha's curse. Somnath temple stands at the shore of the Arabian ocean on the western corner of Indian subcontinent in Gujarat State. This pilgrimage is one of the oldest and finds its reference in the ancient texts like Skandpuran, Shreemad Bhagavat, Shivpuran etc. The hymn from Rig-Veda quoted below mention the Bhagvan Someshwar along with the great pilgrimage like Gangaji, Yamunaji and Eastward Saraswati. This signifies the ancient value of this Theertham.

TEMPLE BUILT

Seen Two renovation, three major invasion of Mogul Kings and many demolition, the 6TH Time built temple gigantically stands in western coast of Gujarat. In 1947 India's iron man Mr. Sardar valabai Patel called on meeting in Ahilyabai temple made a somnath temple trust. It represents Chalukiya architecture. The height of the temple's main shikhara is 155 ft. The kalasam laid on top of the shikhara weighs 10 tons. The flag mast is 37 ft long and one ft. dia.

First time construction-The tradational saying by saints and purna reveals its existance from Vedic period, during Ramayana period the Ravanan made golden temple here, in Mahabarat period **(Duwabra yugam-3150 BC)** Lord Krishna renovated this temple with silver.

Second time construction-In 649 CE, The damaged temple due to aging was built again by Fourth Dhara the grand son of SriHarsh emperor. This temple was demolished by Arabian attacks during 722 CE.

Third time construction-In 800 CE Chalukia kings built the temple with red coloured stones this has been revealed from 960 CE inscriptions.

Fourth time construction-In 1026 CE, The Kajini mohamed from turkey attack the temple with his 30000 horse wariours on 8th january and **killed 50000 somnath region soldier** and enter into the temple Garbagirah broke the lingam into pieces by using Gatha (strong dom like weapon with handle) and taken all valubles like jewels, structural parts made up of gold silver, pearls and Jems. Finally while leaving **set up fire and destroyed the whole temple Fourth time construction-**In 1169 CE **the king Kumarabala** built the temple, the architect**(sathapathi)** named **Pavapra Haspathi** constructed the temple, kept Gold Kalasam on Sikhara top. The **Natrajar statue made**

SOMNATH JOTHIRLINGAM made up of magnetic stones kept **in suspension inside the temple** with a technique of magnetic attraction and repulsion principle

Fifth time construction- In 1300 CE, The delhi sultan **Alahudin kilji's** commanders Alaafkhan, Nusathkhan attach the somnath, killed the Rajputs and enter into the temple. They **broke the lingam inside the Garbagirah, other statues in the temple,** the pieces of broken stones taken to Delhi, their used these stones for laying steps for Mosque. The **Junakath king Mahibalan** renovated the damaged temple and his son **Kenor in 1340 CE,** carry out expansion work in the temple and installed the **largest lingam in its kind** in the Garbagirah and daily ritual worship started in the **Sixth time construction-In 1459 CE, Mohamed saw** the sultan of Gujarat forcibly converted the Hindus in to Muslim and removed the lingam inside the temple converted the Temple into Mosque. But in that place neither Muslim nor Hindus carry out any worship for 3 to 4 centuries, the structure ruined, by the time locals made a small temple outside the town and made worship to Somnath from there. Seeing this helpless situation of Somnath town people, The Indore Queen **Ahilyabai** in 1783 CE constructed new temple for Lord Somnath nearby old temple with two storied type Garbagirah, in that Main lingam kept in underground, the Garbagirah on top floor left blank.

After an India independence The Home minister **Mr. SARDAR VALABAI PATEL made inauguration on 08/05/1950** for temple construction in its original place, the weakened entire old temple structures were removed completely, present new temple was constructed without losing its originality and **Kumbhabisekam has been carried out in May 1965 CE.** And the sacred ceremony of Linga Pratishtha - idol installation was performed by the first President of India, Dr Rajendra Prasad. This temple outer compound wall with Tikvijathwar entrance Gopuram was contructed by **Jamnagar Queen**, remberence to his husband **in 1970 CE.** Sardar valabai patel who took initiation, gathered all people, eventhough amidist opposition, form somnath temple trust and started the somnath temple consturction activites was died in 15/12/1950, to respect his courtesy the statue made up of bronze has been kept in the park just opposite to the temple.

SCUPLTURE WORK IN THE TEMPLE.

It has **155 ft high** main gopuram in vesarah type with Trisol and kalasa on top of Sikhara. The arrow marked in the inner Pragaram represents the southern side there is no land upto the pole of the earth and north side the greater Himalaya and land existance geographically to signify Lord Siva existence every where. The temple is consisting of Garbagirah, Sabhamandap and Nrityamandap with a 150 feet high Shikhar. The Kalash at the top of the Shikhar weighs 10 tons and the Dhwajdand is 27 feet tall and 1 foot in circumference. The shore temple of Somnath is believed to have been built in 4 phases-in gold by Lord Soma, in silver by Ravi, in Wood by lord Krishna and in stone by King Bhimadeva. The existing temple is built in the Kailas Mahameru Prasad style by Sardar valabai patel.

JOURNEY TO THE TEMPLE

From any Major cities in india, train/flight facility available for Ahemadabad/Rajkot. From ahemadabad catch trains to Rajkot. From Rajkot to somnath only one train is there and alight in verraval from their 5 Km on road to Somnath temple. The town has got good lodge/boarding facility you can relax there. The veraval town has got fishing harbor where 4000 power boats involved in fishing. The town has got most sea food processing industry and Aditya birla group rayan industry is there. From veraval bus connectivity to Junagad is ok. From there you can find better bus frequency to various parts of Gujarat. From Nageshwar jothirlingam if you want to come the route is Duwaraka-Jamnagar-porbandar-veraval-Somnath. On road about 380Km.

SAMUDRA MARG:

The Abadhit Samudra Marg, Tirsthambh (Arrow) indicates the un obstructed sea route to the South Pole. The nearest land towards South Pole is about 9936 km. away. This is a wonderful indicator of the ancient Indian wisdom of geography and strategic location of the Jyotirling. The temple renovated by Maharani Ahilyabai is adjacent to the main temple complex

GITA MANDIR:

Bhagavat Gita Slogams were inscripted in big pillars. the other many sculptures were made in small size pillars. Where Lord Krishna and his brother balaraman got Gurukulam education. The Gitamandir is built here where the divine message of Shrimad Bhagavat Geeta is carved on eighteen marble pillars. Shri Lakshminarayan Mandir is close by.

**TRIVENI SANGAMAM
WHERE KRISHNA
FUNNERAL TOOK PLACE**

**BALUKA THEER WHERE
KRISHNA GOT INJURED**

Somnath temple over view

Samudra mark indicated point inside the temple complex:

From this arrow indicated point the light path stretching without obstruction upto the South Pole over the end of the ocean during your visit try to see.

ISTHALAM HISTORY

The Chandira so called as Somon, had married 27 daughters of Mr. Dhaksan, in that he had too much attraction on his two wives, remaining wives were not cared by him much. The Imparity shown by chandira with his other wives made angry of Mr. Dhakson he cursed his son in law. The chandira lost is illumination power due to this curse of his father in law. He tried in many ways the impact of curse should not affect him, he requested Devatas and Brama to give solutions for this problem. As per their advice he reached the earth and take bath in holy place where Saraswathi river mingle with sea called as Prabhasapttinam. He made penance towards lord siva infront of the Hadageshwarar lingam in one leg for about 4000 years to get rid of the curse. During the course of penance he was chanting mantra called IMRUTHUNJA for 10 crores times, Lord Siva declined to the worship made by Moon God(Chandira) and appeared to him as a AGNI form, from Hadageshwarar lingam and blessed the chandira to get back his illumination power on certain condition basis. As per that his illumination power gradually reduces when he is become more weak lord siva protect him by keeping in his head, and enrich the chandira to grow as complete thus the this cycle will repeat. This is the story said for the waxing & waning of the moon, producing new moon & full moon. The chandira (somon) has got back his illumination power in this place hence the place called as Prabhasa (illuminating) isthalam. The Devatas and Brama requested lord siva to extent his grace to all whoever visting this place, considering their request Lord Siva with compassion blessing all of us in the mame of Somanathar in this isthalam. The Rig veda reference also refelect HIM in this place, Lord Siva as a Somanathar, hence the temple called as Somnath temple. Inside the temple you can find old Sakthi temple basement and its ruins.

The temple has got glass showcase gallery in north side walls where the lord siva events from Siva purans where displayed with description for public. The southern side the arrow mark indicator shows from that point the light path stretching without obstruction upto the south pole over the end of the ocean.

PUNIYA THEERTHAM

There are 19 theertham in and around in that following one remarkable due to lord Krishna history behind it. The pond, where Chandra (Moon) took his holy dips during penance is called Somagundam.

ADMINISTRATION

During Chalukia kingdom period from 10000 villages what ever income comes has been utilized for meeting expenses of 1000 Brahamins meant for carrying out pooja, 100 singers, 200 classical dancers and 300 Barbours salary were paid and other rituals activities also taken care. It was the richest temple of those olden days.

OTHER PLACES TO SEE NEAR BY

Chaulika kingdom fort, The ancient Somnath temples recoverd idols and damaged structure kept in musuem inside this fort. **Gita mandir**, sun&chandira temple and other temples of ganesh, and Ahilyabai built somnath temple.

Baluka Tirth.

Where lord Krishna got injured in his right leg. The hunter use the poisoned arrow to hunt a deer, mistakely it pierce into the lord Krishna right leg, the hunter rushed near to krishna with emotionally collapsed and upset condition stand infront of him with wordless. The krishna blessed the hunter with smile and moved from there to **Devosarga** where krishna passedaway.

Trivenisangamam

Where lord Krishna funeral has been carried out. Here three rivers (Saraswati, Hiren and Kamla rivers) joins together in Arabic sea. You can take boat riding from here to sea and have nice view of somnath temple from sea.

BALRAMJIKI GULFA.

The Balramjiki Gufa is the place from where Bhagvan Shrikrishna's elder brother Balaramji took journey to his nijdham-pat. Here is the Parshuram Tapobhumi, where Bhagvan Parshuramji carried out penance and he was relieved from the sin of Kshatriya killings. The Pandavas have said to have visited this place and taken holy bath in the Jalprabhas and built five Shiv temples. The Somnath trust has endeavored to develop the whole Shri Krishna Neejdham Prasthan Tirtha in a wholesome manner in near future.

CEREMONY

The Aarti offering to Lord Somnath while sunset is very special in this temple don't miss it during your visit. Important festival carried out here is 1. Maha sivaratri maha utsav. 2. Golakdham utsav 3. Diwali 4. Shastradeep poojan

Chapter 2.8

TRYAMBAKESHWAR TEMPLE

TRYAMBAKESHWAR TEMPLE MAIN ENTRANCE

**TRYAMBAKESHWAR TEMPLE OVERVIEW AND
ITS BACKGROUND IS BRAMAGIRI HILL**

**GANGA WATER FALLS
IN GODAVARI RIVER**

**PANCAHAVADI IN NASIK
IN GODAVARI RIVER**

If you claim this bramagiri hill throgh steps provided you can find cone like structure where the river godavari originates. The Anjanear statue on the way and saint gouthama with head less cow in his adjacent also on the hill.

KUSHAVARTA KUND:

before entering into the temple devotees should take a dip in this holy kund to purify themselves. Shreemant Rao Sahib Paniker had built the kund banks with stone steps and verandas on all sides.

ORIGIN OF GODAVARI:

While claiming to bhramagiri hills you can find in steps aside Hanumanji icon from this the steps are very steep the tough part of the trekking start to claim the mountain to see Godavari origin at hill top.

TEMPLE BUILT

The original temple was renovated by the Peshwas. The renovation work started by Bajirao and completed by his son **Shrimant Nanasahib Peshwa**. The renovation work strated in the year 26.12.1755 and completed in the year 1785. There were about 768 labors were worked on the temple for a period of thirty one years continuously. They spend Ten lacks during that period for this renovation work.

JOURNEY TO THE TEMPLE:

On temple premise vechile parking facilty available, don't take any body as guide lot of people bluffing in this name. We had reached to the temple 10:0 AM lot of queue was there for Darshan it took around 2 hrs, to get early darshan and to save time strat early queue will be less. From Nasik 28 km by bus,

From Mumbai to Nasik or Pune to Nasik lot of bus/train facility is available.

From Mumbai 3.5Hrs by train on the Way you can find train pass through tunnels and beautiful greenery hill locks. From pune per day only two trains available. If you start from pune better go by pune to nashiq highway road you can find lot of hill locks and fields where onion and perfomogram planted and lot of wind mills on hill tops. High way resturants will fulfill your food need, the hotels are neat and clean. On the way from munchur you can go to Bhimashankar jothir lingam than proceed to nashiq or shridi as per your choice.

ISTHALAM HISTORY

The Gouthama saint lived in Bramagiri hills with his wife Ahgalya. During his period major draught faced by all, due to scarcity of drinking water puplic faced lot of problems and by seeing this situation saint made strong Tabus towards Varuna(God for air) to get rainfall in this region. Varuna reluctant to his request and adviced him to make a pond in that by HIS bless he will get ample amount water. The gouthama executed the same and got good water source from that pond, by utilizing this water he made plantation and thus area become good it attracted all other saints and people to settle in this area. Over a period the settled people had got jealous with Ahagalya and made false complaint against her as she is not allowing others to take water from that pond. This problem aggravated futher, finally the other saints who settled over here decided to push out Saint Gouthama from this place.

In this regard they requested Lord Ganesha to help them out. Lord Ganesha viewed this issue seriouly and finally felt keeping Saint Gouthama inbetween these people will make problem to him to safeguard him he decided to drift him to near by area without hurting him. For this purpose Lord Ganesha manifest himself as COW and went the Gouthama garden and started eating the plants. The Gowtama attempted to ward it off with a bunch of Darbha grass, and caused it the cow to fell down and become unconcious and died. The other saints utilizing this chance and try to expel him from this place quating, Killing Cow causes Gouthma had created sin of Cohati dosam he is not fit to stay in this sacred place. The Gouthama with no other option left from this place and settled in other near by area. The Sin had disturbed him continouly, his concious to come out that he wants to do some Parigaram in this regard he seek the advice of the saints in Brahamagiri hills. As per their advice He made round Brhamagiri hills 11 times and to get ganga water (It is hindus strong belief having bath ganga river water will vanish all our sins and purify us) he and his wife make prayer towards lord Siva, by admiring their prayer Iswar appeared infront of them and ask their need. As per Goutham request Iswar order Ganagdevi to come here and help HIS devotees to get Ganga water.

While Iswar about to leave Ganga requested HIM to stay here permanently as a Jotirling, the mercy Lord Siva accept her request and settle here in Jotirling as Three forms within it.(Brama, Vishnu &siva together). From there the Ganagadevi in the name of Gouthami decend down as Godaviri river from Gangathvaram this origin place called as Triambak.

Tryambakeshwar has been referred in the Padma Purana. The Bhramagiri hill in Tryambakeshwar is referred to in the literature of Marathi saints. The legend relating to the Lingodbhava manifestation of Shiva also prevails here. Legend has it that Brama and Vishnu searched in vain to discover the origin of Shiva who manifested himself as a cosmic column of fire. Brama lied that he had seen the top of the column of fire, and was hence cursed that he would not be worshipped on earth. In turn Brama cursed Shiva that he would be pushed underground. Accordingly, Shiva came down under the Bhramagiri hill in the form of Tryambakeshwar. Circumambulating the Bhramagiri hill is considered sacred. (Please also see the Arunachala Hill, and the legend associated with the Origin of Linga worship).

SCULPTURE WORK IN THE TEMPLE

This temple built up of blak stone in the Nagara style of architecture with in a spacious courtyard. The sanctum internally a square and externally a stellar structure houses a small Shivalingam - Tryambaka. The sanctum top and crowned with a graceful tower and its peak crowned with a giant golden kalasha. In front of the Garbagirah and the antarala mandap have doors on all four sides. Three of these doorways are covered with porches, and the openings of these porches are ornamented with pillars and arches. The roof of the mandapam is formed by curvilinear slabs rising in step by steps. The entire structure is ornamented with sculptural work featuring running scrolls, flowery designs, figures of gods, yakshas, humans and animals. The temple built in the Indo Aryan style. The temple structure with excellent adornments of idols and sculptures is surrounded by a massive black stone wall. There is a huge bull in front of the temple and another marble Nandi is kept in the inside.

From the Jyotir Lingam at the centre of the Garbagirah, trickles the Ganges continuously throughout the year. When I visit recently on Apl.2014 from the linga no water comes out i could observe the linga in wet form. The Garbagirah arthamandapam Dom constructed in 16 segments, it has four entrances, eight nos arch like structure to support the Dom from the base.

PUNIYA THEERTHAM:

Here the Ganga (Godavari) appeared and reappeared several times in response to the please of Gowtama Rishi, and there are several theerthas associated with this temple. The Gangadwara theertha is believed to be the site where Ganga emerged. Varaha theertha is where Vishnu in the form of Varaaha took a bath in the Ganga (Godavari).

The Kushavarta theertha is a pond with steps on all sides, with pillared aisles with highly ornate arches. This is considered to be the holiest of all the theerthas here, and is believed to be the spot where Gowtama Rishi finally secured Ganga on earth. The structure around this theertha was constructed by Raoji Abaji Parnekar of the Holkars of Indore in 18th century.

Other thirthas here are the Gangasagar the Gautamalaya, Bilva theertha, Indra theertha,

Vishwanath theertha, Mukund theertha, Prayag theertha, Rama Kund, Lakshmana Kund. The confluence of the rivers Ahalya and Godavari is also you can see here.

CEREMONY.

During auspicious time the linga has been crowned with three murthi idol which is made up of silver, during your visit try to see this. I could not able to see the same in my last visit time. Shivalingam is covered with a silver mask, and on festive occasions with a golden mask with five faces, each with a golden crown. The Brahamins sit inside the Artha mandapam makes special pooja on demand of course you have to pay money. Three worship services are carried out each day. During the nightly worship service sheja-aarti is carried out and the silver mask is placed in a bed in the hall of mirrors. Each Monday, the silver mask of Tryambaka is placed in a palanquin and taken in procession to Kushavarta theertha and given an abhisheka there. This procession with the special golden mask happens also on Shiv ratris, full moon day in the month of Kartika and during other festive occasions.

Simhasta Parvani which occurs once in a every 12 year a great festivity event here. The Ganga avatarana festival is celebrated during the month of Magha, it is believed all the heavenly Gods grace promised to come down to Nasik during this period, once in twelve years, when Jupiter resides in the zodiac sign of Leo during Kumbamela festivel.

OTHER PLACES TO SEE NEAR BY

Ganga water falls, Water theme park near tryambakeshwar temple, Balaji mandir and someshwar mandir where boating facility available, panchavadi where lakshmana reka where sita has been abducted by ravana, other temples closely located here are sita kund, ram kund, kala ram Ghora ram, Bhakthi dam, Mukthidam seet gupha, shiv mandir, kapaleshwar mandir kapila Godavari sangamam and pandulena caves in mahendravadi hills.

END OF CHAPTER 2.8

Chapter 2.9

KUSHMESHWAR OR GRISHNESHWAR TEMPLE

This Jyotir Lingam exists at Devagiri near Ellora. The Lord is known by several names - Kusumeswar, Ghushmeswara, Grushmeswara, and Grishneswara. Grishneshwar Jyotirlinga Shrine is a temple located in verul village just 1km fom the vicinity of the tourist town of Ellora, 30km from Aurangabad, 186Km from Nashiq railway station and 110Km from Shridi. The Grishneswar temple is also familiarly known as Kushmeshwar

TEMPLE BUILT

The temple was initially built by Rastrakuda kings who ruled this region in those days. The Thandidurga and Krishnaraya kings combinely renovated this temple in 750 CE. Latter on in 14th century the rich people overhere did some renovation work and made pooja here. In between this period it subject to more Mugual attacks and finally the Delhi sultan completely destroyed this. The destroyed temple was again built by Chatrapathi Sivaji's grandfather and Saduvithdoshi Baba effort again the Mugal king Aurangasip destroyed this temple. In 1730 CE the Madavarao Holkar's wife Gowthamiboy built this present day temple in 240ft X 185 ft size with red color stones. In 1769 CE the Sivalaya Pushkarani (Holy Pond) renovation work carried out by Queen Ahilyabai who also reconstructed the Kasi Viswanatha temple at Varanasi and the Vishnu Paada temple at Gaya. The pushkarani extent in 185 Sq. Ft. It has got 56 step respectively in four sides to reach water level. In water level it has got 8 small temple which indicates 8 theerthams over here.

JOURNEY TO THE TEMPLE

From Mumbai or surat or nasik or any major cities you can reach Aurangabad by train. From their towards Dhulobath about 30 Km near by ELORA get down at Verul village to see this temple. We had reached to the temple about 1pm got darshan in 45 minutes. The gents were asked to remove the shirt before entering in to the Garbagirah this is the tradition followed here. All are allowed to touch linga and do pooja in their own. While coming from pune take diverson at singanapur where nasik, Mumbai, pune and shridi going junction met point take diversion route to shridi, after your shridi visit you can proceed from shridi to ellora than Aurangabad. From ellora to Aurangabad route you can find good hill locks, Aurangazip fort, dulatabad fort, bird sanactury, water theme park, in Aurangabad you can see mini taj mahal, Aurangabad caves, than proceed to Ajanta caves.

ISTHALAM HISTORY

In the present Maharastra near Devagiri hills in Bharatvaja village the Sudarma and his wife Sudeka lived together. They were doing lot of good deeds to all people and their life style is very simple and marvelous it becomes a exemplary life to all of them. He was a great devotee of Siva. He was not blessed with a son. In that village people keep on abuse Sudeka about her infertiltiy due to this she broke out and told to her husband I can't leave with this blame better I will die instead of living like this life. The Sudarma convinced her regularly if god made certain things it had got some meaning in that, HE want us not to have bondage with this worldly life, Hence we will make regular worship to HIM to attain MUKTHI. But sudeka forced her husband to marry her brother daughter named Kushma. At the persuasion of his family and his first wife, he got married to Kusuma, in order to give him a son. Kusuma was an even greater devotee of Lord Siva. Everyday she would make one Siva Linga, worship it and then immerse it in the temple pond. The Kushma daily makes lingam from soil after pooja she dissolve the same in a pond near to their house, over a period it had crossed more than lack by seeing her strong devotion Lord Siva bless her to have a child.

The Kushma has got cute boy, she named him as Supriyan. The all village people came and see the child and praised the Kushma in many ways. The Sudarma also take care child and Kushma well, these all things created jealous in Sudeka mind towards Kusma and her child. Over a period the Supriyan had got marriage with beautiful girl and lead happy life over here. Eventhough every body takes care her well the jealous in Sudeka mind keep on aggravated and she felt alone and depressed at one stage and the rootcause for all these to happen is due to her Step child hence she decided to kill him. One day she killed Supriyan by using axe while he is sleeping with his wife and cut his body into many pieces and thrown his body into the pond where Kusma use to disolve her worshiped lingam.

The sudarma and kushma finished their pooja and came to their house saw the situation over there, the supriyan wife revealed them all the incidents. The sudarma visualize the pathetic condition of his family members and try to Console them, with confident he expressed getting back his son again not in our hand, the almighty will take care us, let us continue our pooja towards HIM. Kusuma was deeply grieved, yet did not stop her daily worship of Lord Siva. She continued to make the Lingam, worshipped & immersed it in the pond.

**KUSHMESHWAR
TEMPLE OVERVIEW**

**SHRIDI SANCTRAM
INSIDE VIEW**

**KAILASH TEMPLE MADE BY CARVING STONE IT IS
WORLD LARGEST MONOLITHIC STONE TEMPLE**

To the surprise of one and all, her son rose out of the water one day, coming back to life. Kushma rushed to her son and hug him very happily whilst from that pond with powerful illumination, by your eyes you cant see this light with such a light intensity the Jothirlingam appeared there, from that the Lord Siva came out and give HIS darshan to them. By seeing this unexpected Darshan both of them laid down towards his feet and made their worship to Lord Siva and requested HIM to stay here permanently and Give HIS blessings to all who come here, the Siva accepted their deep request and settle in that Jothirlingam and giving darshan to all of us now also.

SCUPLTURE WORK

24 Pillar halls (Saba), The Dhasa Avathar of vishnus, Big tortise and Beautiful Nandi located towards the direction of Garbagirah, The good workman ship Sikhara you must see while returning.

PUNIYA THEERTHAM-Sivalaya theertham.

OTHER PLACES TO SEE NEAR BY

Ellora temple which has several rock cut monuments from the 1st millennium and have beautiful kailash temple in cave no.16, other jain temple, etc. The ellora has got total 32 nos caves. Hanuman, Bhadra maruti and Biravar temple in verul, Aurangabad and its caves, Ajanta caves 3 hrs drive from here.

END OF CHAPTER 2.9

Chapter 2.10

GOD NAME-BIMASANKAR, GODESS NAME-KAMALAJA

TEMPLE SANCTRUM
DEVOTEES OFFERING
TO LINGA

TEMPLE ENTRANCE

MATAJI TEMPLE IN BIMASANKAR

DIMPEY DAM ON THE WAY TO BIMASANKAR

This Jyotirlinga Shrine is associated with the legend of Shiva destroying the demon Tripurasura. Lord Siva is considered to be taking rest here after the Trpurantaka samharam. The sweat drops of Lord Siva were converted as steam and running from here as Bhima river. In temple premises Backside of the temple you can find holy spring.

New structures have been added. There are two idols of Nandideva. One idol is old, while the other is of fairly recent addition. There is a theertham & a well behind the temple structure. Bhimashankar is located in the Sahyadri hills of Maharashtra, accessed from Pune. The entrance is flanked by a statue of Nandi. There is also a small shrine of Shani Dev inside the temple. The sacred Shiva Linga is placed on the center of Garbagirah's floor.

TEMPLE BUILT

As per the facts available, the Adams carried out pooja and made small temple in this place, over the period stage by stage the temple was built, In **Peshwa period** the full temple was completed. The ritual pooja were strated. In 1733 AD; The Simaanaji sundaji Patnayak kind renovated the temple. In 1766 AD Thidchithpatavarthan carry out some repair works. The marata **king Chatrapthi Shivaji** offer the KAROSI village incomes as endowment to meet this temple day to day expenses. Presently the steps and its corridor and temple renovation work is going on.

SCUPLTURE WORK IN THE TEMPLE.

The wooden carvings in doors and vidhana and inside roof supports made nicely. In compound wall it depicts the Ramayana, krishnalilai and sivalilai It scene's. In Garbagirah the lingam height is 40cm, during pooja time it will be decorated marvelously and covered by Gold made **PANCHA MOGA lingam**, the original shape of main lingam not visible to us. Bhimashankar temple with its Indo Aryan and Nagra style of architecture was built by Nana Fadnis.

JOURNEY TO THE TEMPLE

This temple has been located in deep forest area called as **POVAGIRI** range, **3000 ft high** from sea level. From pune 96 km by bus, through dense forest travel will excite us, you can find wild animals on the way. There are lot of sign board on the road beware wild animals where it may cross the road. It has got two hill resorts nearby to stay and watch this beautiful locations. We had reached 1pm to the temple the stair case leading from parking area to temple quite deep aged people better utilize dolly available on hire basis. In Garbagirah all devotees allowed to touch linga and pay their offering, we could able to see god without much queue here, for darshan hardly it took few minutes. Near by temple small village available and lot of small chatirams available There is no good lodge facility available, the maharastra tourism department constructing good guset house like in ellora once it comes into service we could able to stay safely in temple near.

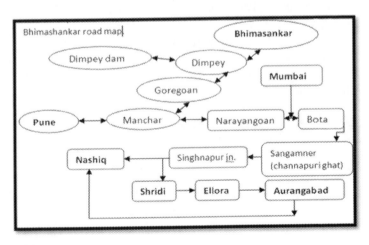

Bhimashankar road map

If you come from Mumbai, the nearest station from which buses ply is Karjat. Enroute one can be embraced by Ganesh Ghat or Shidi Ghat. Both the ways are a bit tough but at the same time enjoyable. If the dense forest route is taken, then you have to travel for 4 hours to reach to the top. According to mythology these forests were once trekked by the Pandavas of the Indian epic Mahabharata.

PUNIYA THEERTHAM:

The temple near by **Beema River** originates from the **Motcha kondam** and flow downwords and mingle with Chandirabhaga River.

ISTHALAM HISTORY

The sri langa king Ravanan and his brother Kumbagarnan and his son beema lived in Ramayana period. The katkadi lives in hill range(Presnt pune hiils range called as POVAGIRI) alone, there she had made Kandarva vivakam(one type of marriage method) with kumbargana, after few month he proceed to langa and left her alone while she was pregnant. After few months she had birth of son called beema. They were lived in this place, upon beema growing elder, he started asking about his father details. She revealed her life tragedy to him. Her first husband named VIRATHAN and second husband KUMBAKARNA both have been killed by Rama in battle, by hearing this Beemasuran had got more angry on Lord Rama and decided to kill HIM. To increase his strength he made tabus vigrously towards Brama standing on one leg over many years, Brama appeared infront of him and accepted his request and offered a boon of being a strongest and powerful warior. He is basically RAKSAS in nature he misused his power and strated torturing all kind of people who lived in the society. Not allowing any one to make spritual worshhip, to conduct yagnam, yaga and omum. The irritated groups of brahamins, saints, rishis and all afected people gathered together in Mahakosa river and made pray to god to overcome from this situation. Considering these devotees deep prayer Lord siva given assurance to all of them his end of days were counted he will be killed soon. Wherever he won the battle the defeated kings taken into custody in prison, out of which one of the king Priya dharman and his wife dhakshini were in prison worshiped the linga made up of soil with deep trust on Lord regularly.

One day this couple in deep pooja, the beemasuran came to the prison and warned them to stop the pooja, but priya dharman continued his pooja, the irritated king pull out his sword and approach the king near. The Priya Dharman wife Dhakshini made loud nice O my god save my husband, by hearing her words from lingam one NAGABASAM appeared and destryoed the sword in his hand and from ASHRI voice HE warned the Beemasuran to give up his worst behaviours but he is not in the mood to listen HIS words. In the meanwhile the saint NARATHA came to this spot and pray towards ishwar and requested HIM to SAMHARA this cruiel beemasuran. Considering his request the iswar came out from this lingam in AGNI form, not withstanding this heat Beemasuran and all his soldiers were died. The all devotees of Maheshwar requsted with deep worship to stay in this place permanently and to give his JOTHIRLINGA darsan to everyone who comes to this sacred place, iswar consider their request and become BEEMASANKARAR in this sacred place.

OTHER PLACES TO SEE NEARBY:

In Mahabaleshwar the following things can be seen Religious-Lord Karthikeya Temple, Panchgani, Mahabaleshwar Temple and krishnai temple

Rajpuri Caves, Panchgani

The Rajpuri Caves in Panchgani is a religiously important tourist spot. These ancient caves are surrounded by many water kunds (ponds). Devotees believe that taking bath in these holy kunds will provide relief from all kinds of diseases and evils. Legends claim that the holy Ganges also flows into that.

Historical things of Mahabaleshwar.

Kamalgad Fort, Panchgani **Morarji Castle** Another worthy to watch spectacle in the hilly terrain of Mahabaleshwar is the Morarji Castle. An old structure that reflects the influence of the British style architecture, Morarji Castle allures the onlookers with its glittering appeal. As a part of the freedom struggle Gandhiji came to Mahaba leshwar.

Mount Malcolm

John Malcom was one among the illustrious generals of the British troops. In 1828 he came to Mahabaleswar and he was very much impressed by the scenic charm of Mahabaleshwar. In fond remembrance of this great man, the most fabulous mansion of the colonial era was named after him. Mount Malcom

Pratapgad Fort

The Pratapgad Fort is the place from where the history of the Maratha Emperor Shivaji turned into a decisive course. This is here that Afzal Khan met his death. The Pratapgad Fort is 900 m above sea level. It is 24 km west of Mahabaleshwar. The fort from a distance gives the appearance of a round

NATURE

Arthur's seat, Babbington Point, Bombay Point (Sunset Point) Carnac Point, Chinaman's Falls, Connaught Peak, Dhobi Waterfall Elephant's Head Point, Elphinstone Pointt, Falkland Point, Helen's Point Hunter Point, Kate's Point, Lingmala Falls, Lodwick Point, Marjorie Point Parsi Point-Panchgan,

Serbaug-Panchgani, Tableland-Panchgani, Tiger's Spring Venna Lake, and Wilson Point (Sunrise Point).

PLACE TO SEE IN PUNE IN AND AROUND

Siddi vinayak temple, Devi temple in hill lock and OSHO ashram, Lonavala, khandala caves and Mahabaleshwar.

END OF CHAPTER 2.10

Chapter 2.11

SRI SAILAM TEMPLE

Godname-**Maligarjunar,**Godessname-**Bramarambaigai**.
It is one of the **Devaram Rymes** sang isthalam. State-
Andhra pradesh. The **LINGAM** height is **25cm** only, anyone
can go near and make worship to god by offering vilva leaves
and flowers. West side of the siva shrine devi shrine is there,
the hole in the wall behind devi shrine keep your ears you will
hear Rithamic sound of flying insects. The temple is situated
facing East. The centre mandapam has sveral pillars, with a
huge idol of Nandikeswarar. Ambal's sannadhi is to the west
of Iswaran Sannadhi. River Krishna runs along the foothills.
Since it runs through deep valley during parts of its journey, It
is known as Paadaala Gangai. Devotees believe in a darshan of
the the Sri Saila Sikaram from the Sikareswarar temple situated
six miles from Sri Sailam.

Apart from this you can see indivudal shrines for
Ganapathi, Arumugan, sakaskara lingam (where Lord Rama
made pooja), chandravathi's maligarjunar, Rajarajeshwarar,
Rajarajeshwari, Veerabadraswami and isaptha mathkal. The
east pragaram has got pancha nandis instaled against each
lingam.

TEMPLE BUILT

It is ancient temple as per inscription it was built in 1230 AD by Myla Mahadevi a KAKATIYA princess, In 1674 AD. The **Maratha warior veera shivaji** visited this temple and built the temple north entrance gopuram. The Garbagirah contains a naturaly formed Shiva linga which devotees are permitted to touch. It has been constructed in the traditional Dravidian style. This shrines along with Thiruppudaimarudur near Ambasamudram and thiruvidai marudur is considered an Arjuna Shetram. The three Saivaite saints Thiruganasambandar, Thirunavukkarasar and Sundarar have sung in praise of this Lord. Adi Sankarar is said to have composed the Sivananda Lahari at this isthalam. The presiding deities are Mallikarjunar and Brahmaramba. Lord Nandikeswarar in the form of a mountain is considered to be holding up Lord Siva. Mallikarjunam has been mentioned in the Thevaram as Paruppadam. The lord is hence known as Paruppadanayagan & the Devi Paruppadanayagi. The theertham is known as Paruppadatheertham. The temple surrounded by mountains called Nandi hills, Nandial and Navanandi this mouintain area called **Pookailasam.** Srisailam comprises 9 mountain peaks, 9 Holy river, 9 caves, 9 towns, 9 holy theertham and 9 religious leaders

SRISAILAM MAIN TEMPLE OVER VIEW.

BADALA GANGA

SIKARA VIEW POINT

TEMPLE SCULPTURE WORK

The temple has got 20 ft high gijantic compound wall in that the purna events carved nicely. In Bottom two rows horse, elephant and war scene were depicted, on top two rows Arujuna tabus, Chandiravathi history, Parvathi pariyanam, rishis worship to siva, margandeyan story, Dhaksha yognam and different murtis of lord siva carved.

JOURNEY TO THE TEMPLE

To reach srisailam from Guntakal, Guntur, Karnool, Mahanandi, vijawada, hyderabad, ananthpur and thriupati bus services available. From chennai to vijawada train route alight at Ongole station from their 180 km by bus. From DURNA the hill route start you can find marvelous sceneray and landscape on the way. At 12 km ahead to srisailam the place sikareshwaram from this peak(476 M High from ground level), the beautiful view of temple and krishna reservoir takes you a into different feeling. On 5km ahead to temple you can find SATCHI(WITNESS) VINAYAR temple. It is believed he note down the devotee's details in his OLAYCHUVADI.

From Vijawada on road 250km it tooks around 8 hours by bus. From Dornala the Arch welcomes you to srisailam. At foot of the hills the APSTC (Andhra Pradesh tourism lodge available) in dornala itself few lodge available. From Dornala the hill root for 45km to reach temple. Just 5KM ahead to temple the root get divert for Sunny benta where The Wild life Environment education center, Tiger project center park and Ecological environment study centre are there. On the way The Chenchu Tribal museum is there if you have time visit the same. The most of the devotees from Andra Pradesh and karntaka. For free Darshan it took around 3 hrs on busy saturady. Apart from this the Rs.100 and 500 darshan are there if you want to have early Darshan you can utilize this counter.

At Srisailam nearby temple lot of Sadans (accommodation facilty) available, to stay there one can book the rooms stay comfortably in hill top itself. In Siva temple normaly the Hair offering by head shave not found but here Devotees offer their hair to Maligarjuna Swamy. This tradition might have originated by Reddy's in this area.

ISTHALAM HISTORY

When Siva and Parvathi decided to find suitable brides for their sons, Ganesha and Muruga argued as to who is to get wedded first. Lord Siva bade that the one who goes round the world in Pradakshinam could get married first. By the time Lord Muruga could go round the world on his vahana, Lord Ganesha went round his parents 7 times (for according to Sastras, going in Pradakshinam round one's parents is equivalent to going once round the world (Boopradakshinam). Lord Siva got Siddhi & Buddhi, the daughters of Viswaroopan married to Lord Ganesha.

Muruga on his return was enraged and went away to stay alone on Mount Kravunja in the name of Kumarabrahmachari. On seeing his father coming over to pacify him, he tried to move to another place, but on the request of the Devas, stayed closeby. The place where Lord Siva and Parvathi stayed came to be known as Sri Sailam. Lord Siva visits Lord Muruga on Amavasai day & Parvathi Devi on Pournami.

The another legend behind this temple is as follows. Chandiraguptan who ruled north side of Krishna river bank, return back from battles after several years of war. While returning to his motherland on the way he found beautiful girl name called Chandiravathi (His own daughter) admired by her beauty he forcibly want her. She revealed I am your own daughter pl. leave me such a informal relation against Dharma I never agree, tactfully she escaped from him and cross the Krishna river and settled in southern side of Krishna river adjacent hill area. She has got some cows and goat to lead her life in this forest, in that one cow never gives milk she watched that particular cow activites and followed its all activity. One day at evening she observed while returning to hut on the way this cow pierce out all its milk on top of the **soil heap,** next day morning with some people help she excavate the soil heap their they found SUAMBU lingam, upon seeing all were chant **sambo Mahadeva, Sambo Mahadeva** repeatedly and pray to **HIM(linga)** vigorously. The locals decided to remove the linga from there and to install in other good place to make worship regularly, but they were not able to even shack the lingam, utterly failed to remove the sacred lingam. From that day onwards Chandravathi daily made milk Abisakem to this JOTHIRLINGAM and maintain well this sacred place. One day lord siva came in her dream and ask her to offer Jasmine Garland daily to HIM, from that onwards with jasmine garland she make worship to HIM daily. In local language (TAMIL) jasmine flower called as Maligai hence the god also called as Malligarjunar. As per lord instruction to her in dream, she made small temple called MANDAPAM in that place she attained sacred death over the period. Hear tradiationally during pooja ladies are throwing VENSAMARAM to the lord and paying tributes to HIM.

PUNIYA THEERTHAM:

The krishna river flows north and west side of Srisailam this is called as **BADALA GANGAI**, To reach this 5KM distance from hill Cable car facility and 1000 steps are provided to reach this theertham (the wide reservoir buit in the krishna river valley, will jeal you to have a boating in this place. Paltara and Panchatara where Adisankarar made tabus while his visit, the pal falls nowdays not visible.

VEERA SORA MANDAPAM

This Mandapam located in between Nandhi mandapam and Artha mandapam just before to Garbagirah. According to inscription this Mandapam was built by Annavera reddy of Reddy kings in 1378 AD for attaining Puniya of his parental uncle Anna reddy. Srisailam played a dominant role in our religious, cultural and social history from ancient times.

The epigraphical evidence reveals that the history of Srisailam begins with the Sathavahanas who were the first empire builders in South India. The earliest known historical mention of the Hill - Srisailam, can be traced in Pulumavis Nasik inscription of 1st Century A.D.

The Sathavahanas, the Ikshavakus, the Pallavas, the Vishnukundis, the Chalukyas, the Kakatiyas, the Reedy Kings, the Vijayanagara Emperors and Chatrapathi Shivaji are among the famous emperors who worshipped God Mallikarjuna Swamy. Prataparudra of Kakatiya Dynasty strived a lot for the improvements of this Kshetram and granted Paraganas for its maintenance. Ganapathideva has spent 12000 Golden Nanyas for the maintenance of the temple.

The period of Reddi Kings is the Golden Age of Srisailam that almost all rulers of the dynasty did celebrated service for this temple. In 14th Century Prolaya Vema Reddi of Reddy Dynasty constructed stepped path-way to Srisailam and Pathalaganga (Here the river Krishna is called as Pathalaganga) and Anavema Reddi constructed Veera Siromandapam in which the Veerasaiva devotees cut off their hands, tongue, limbs with devotion to attain the realisation of the God. This practice is known as Veeracharam.

The Second Harihararaya of Vijayanagara Empire constructed the Mukhamantapam of Swamy shrine and also a Gopuram on Southern Side of the temple. In the 15th Century Sri Krishnadevaraya Constructed the Rajagopuram on Eastern side and Salumantapas on both sides of the temple. The last Hindu King who strove hard for the improvement of the temple is Chatrapathi Shivaji who constructed a Gopuram on northern side.

FAMOUS CERMONY:

Mahasivaratri, Magrashanranthy and telugu new year lot of devotees will come here. On sivaratri day **the 180 Meter length white cloth decorated** from bottom to Gopura and nandimandapa in beautiful way like netcell, every one can visulaize during their visit. This sacred cloth distributed to devotees as Prasath on completion of function.

The saint saying
Have a Aruthra darshan in Chidambaram
Have a vaikonda agadesi darshan in Sri Rangam
Have a karthigai Deepa darshan in thiruvanamalai
Have a sivaratri darshan in Srisailam

OTHER PLACES TO SEE

Chandira kundam, Rudratcha mandapam, saranga mandapam, Panchaasri mandapam, cokarpam, Kandaa mut, Elephant Lake, Baadala ganga, Lingalapattu and Narasimarpilam.

Opposite to the Sakshi Ganapathi temple in the steps you can proceed to the Balathara spring(Milky spring) and Panchathaara (Sugar spring), where the Adisankarar made penance and Hatekeshwarar temple you can find. For going to these three places lot JEEP trips available from Srisailam. Paltara and Panchatara where Adisankarar made penance during his visit.

Tripurantakam temple to the east.
Siddavatam temple of the Cuddapah district to the South.
Alampur Navabhrama temples in Mahboobnagar district to the West.
Umamaheswaram in Mahboobnagar district to the North are considered as **entrance to Srisailam** in those respective directions.

Few prominets mutts that expels the religious activity.

- Paladhara Panchadara : The spot where Adi Sankara is said to have meditated.
- Hatakeswaram: Another Shiva temple near Paladhara Panchadara where the lingam was originally made of gold.
- Sackshi Ganapathi temple: It is considered important to visit this temple before visiting Sri Sailam.

MALIGARJUNAR JOTHIRLINGAM

- Kailasa Dwaram : The main entrance to Sri Sailam for those trekking to the temple.
- Sikharam : There is a hill temple dedicated to Shiva at a height of 2850 feet above sea level in the Nallamalai hills.
- Patalaganga : is where the bathing ghats associated with Sri Sailam are located. (Krishna River).

TEMPLE ADMINISTRATION

The temple pooja's work taken care by Mysore Lingaya generation tradiationally. Anyone can pay homage to the god directly by touching lingam.

END OF CHAPTER 2.11

Chapter 2.12

RAMESHWARAM TEMPLE

God name- **Ramanathar**, Godess name-**Pervatha varthini.**

The temple total area is 15 Acre. The temple extent is North to south-657 ft. and east to west 865 ft. very large temples among jothirling shrines. This shrine is located at the extreme south eastern point of the Indian peninsula. The Sethu Bridge was constructed to link this land to Lanka for the Vanarams to reach Lanka. This island temple resembles the Panchajanya (Vishnu's conch) and like the Tamil letter 'OM'.

It is a huge structure with three parakarams and several mandapams with mini shrines to other deities. There is a huge Anjaneya in a mini shrine. There is a huge Nandi measuring 12 feet in length and 9 feet in height with the idols of Viswanatha Naicker and Krishnama Naicker. There are shrines for Ganapathi and Subramanya. To the right of the Lord's shrine is the shrine for Parvathi to its North The other Shrines inside the temple are Santhana Ganapathi, Pallikonda perumal, Sethu madavar, Natrajar, Mahalakshmi and Visalatchi. **TEMPLE BUILT** Initially the Garbagirah was built in 12th century by Sri langa king Parakgrama Pagu, later on 15th century the other sannathis were built by Ramanathapuram king Udayar sethupathi, than sucessive sethupathi kings were completed full temple by 18th cetury with some donation received from Devakottai jaminthars.

TEMPLE SCULPTURE WORK

The temple has got three Prakaras in these the third one having 1212 pillars and extent by 30 ft. X 60 ft. with Marvelous sculpture work in each pillar's to be seen in our lifetime. The corridor is the longest one in Asia. It is 197 metres on East-West, 133 metres inlength on South-North.

TEMPLE HISTORY

Lord Rama defeated the Ravanan, and made the Vibushnan as a sri lanka king. The sin(Brahamahati dhosa) caused by kill of Ravanan by Ramar has to be purified. The jyotirlingam was worshipped by Lord Rama to atone the sin of killing Ravana. Hanuman flew to bring the Linga from Kailasa, for Lord Rama to wroship. As it was getting late, Rama installed the Lingam that was made of sand by Sita Devi. This Lingam worshipped by Lord Rama is known as Ramanathar. The Rama had made holy well called as AGNITHEERTHAM with this water he made ABISEKAM to RAMALINGAM.

When Hanuman returned he was disappointed that his Lord had not used the Lingam that he had brought. The Hanuman not convinced with Rama request, finally Rama allowed Hanuman to deinstall the RAMALINGAM. The Hanuman tried with his tail, finally he got injured and become unconscious and the holy tears of Rama fall on Hanuman and recovered him. Rama had blessed the Hanuman, henceforth your blood stagnant this place will be called as HANUMANTH KUNDAM. Lord Rama pacified Hanuman & named this Lingam as Kasi Viswanathar and allowed him to install his lingam north side of the Main lingam, this LINGAM called as VISWANATHAR. Devotees have to worship Kasi Viswanathar before worshipping Ramanathar.

Thousands of people perform rituals in the sacred corridors of the Rameshwaram temple everyday. It is said that all the rivers of India had come down to Rameshwaram on Lord Ram`s request. Thus the temple has over 100 wells having waters from all the rivers. Devotees take a bath from all these wells and then sit down, purified, for the rituals. The rituals are mostly performed for the purificatiton of oneself and also of his or her ancestors.People from all over the india comes here for dissolving their ancestor hasti in the sea. The recent Sharukkhan film Chennai express it has been revealed nicely the movie reveals while taking hasti from north to south india what are all the things happening and finally how he dissolved his grand mother hasti into sea with that claimax the film end.

PUNNIYA THEERTHAMS

This temple has got total of 51 theerthams, 22 of them situated within the temple among that 25 Nos remarkable one listed in the below table. Pilgrimage is considered complete with a bath in the Agni theertham. These waters are considered to have medicinal qualities.

Sl. No	Inside temple theertham	outside temple theertham
1	Codi theertham	Agni theertham
2	Sarva theertham	Dhanuskodi theertham
3	Sathyamirtha theertham	Rama theertham
4	Siva theertham	Lakshmana theertham
5	Gaya theertham	Sita theertham
6	Yamuna theertham	Hanumanth theertham
7	Ganga theertham	Sukriva theertham
8	Chandira theertham	Vibushna theertham
9	Suriya theertham	Jada theertham
10	Brahmahati vimocha theertham	Lakshmi theertham
11	Sakra theertham	Agni theertham
12	Sangu theertham	Brama kundam
13	Neela theertham	Amirthavabi
14	Nala theertham	Mangala theertham
15	Kavaba theertham	Vedala theertham
16	Suvatcha theertham	Pabavimochna theertham
17	Kanthamaathana theertham	Kabala theertham
18	Sethu mathava theertham	Manasa theertham
19	Saraswati theertham	Sura kundam
20	Gathri theertham	Kabi kundam
21	Savithri theertham	Rinamochna kundam
22	Mahalakshmi theertham	Pandava theertham
23		Deva theertham
24		Upavithanthra theertham
25		Agasthiya theertham

In this the sea in front of the temple is Agni theertham (Having bath in this liberates from Brahamahati dhosam)and the sea in Dhanuskodi is Dhanuskodi thertham.(Having bath in this place will sacred you equivalent to the staying in powerful siva temple for one year).

The procedure to take path in all respective theertham in order is lengthy one. The practice is have a bath first in **Agni theertham, than remaining 27 important theertham and end up in CODI theertham than visit Main lingam.** **CEREMONY** Every Friday the sakthi is procession inside the temple in PALLAK which is made up of gold is to be seen by every one. This temple is famous for ritual HASTI DILUTION of ancestor.

OTHER PLACES TO SEE

Also visit Gandhamathana Parvatham, a hillock, 3kms north of the temple. It is where Lord Rama's feet is found as an imprint on a Chakra.

END OF CHAPTER 2

Chapter 3

ASTATASA SAKTHI PEEDAMS

18 Sakthi peedams considered holy in an India where Devi Body parts fallen during RUDRA thandavam of Siva carried out. Devi Name Location of the temple.

1. Sangari	- Srilanka
2. Kamatchi	- Kanchipuram, Tamilnadu
3. Sirungala	- Prathuim, West Bengal
4. Samundi	- Mysore, Karnataka
5. Jogulambal	- Alampuram, Andhra Pradesh
6. Bramarambal	- Srisailam, Andhra Pradesh
7. Puruhothiga	- Pedapuram, Andhra Pradesh
8. Manickambal	- Dratcharam, Andhra Pradesh
9. Mahalakshmi	- Kollapur, Maharastra
10. Egavera	- Makuram, Maharastra
11. Mahakali	- Ujjain in Madiya Pradesh
12. Girija devi	- Otiyana, Odisha
13. Kamarubi	- Guwathi, Assam
14. Madavi	- Prayag, Uttar Pradesh

15. Visalatchi	- Kasi, Uttar Pradesh
16. Vaisnavi	- Juwalamuki, Jammu
17. Mangal Gowri	- Gaya, Bihar
18. Saraswati Devi	- Kashmir.

END OF CHAPTER 3

Chapter 4

A VISIT TO INDIAN TEMPLES STATE WISE. TAMILNADU TEMPLES

In this below tablur column for visiting the temple in order, I had made Sl. no arrangement in such a way one can travel through shorter way if you start from Chennai to southmost part of tamilnadu. The Sub serial number has been given inorder to see the group of near by temple located in that locality. For example Sl. No.1 to 1.4 refers Chennai temples.

TAMILNADU SHIVA TEMPLES TRAVEL GUIDE

	Origin Town	Temple town	Via	KM	Temples on the way (Brown one are 108 siva temples)
1	1. Chennai central	1. Tiruninravur	Avadi	29	Irudhyaliswarar
2	1.1. Tiruninravur	1.1. Tiruvaluvar	Avadi	13	
3	1.2. Tiruvaluvar	1.2. Chennai	Avadi	42	
4	1.3. Chennai koyambedu	1.3. Mylapore	Anand theatre	16	**Kabaliswarar, Vellishwar**
5	1.4. Mylapore	1.4. Thiruvanmiur	Manthaivelly	7	Sri Maruntheshwarar
6	2. Chennai	2. Suratapalli	Towards thirupathi route		**Palli kondiswar**
7	3. Chennai	3. Kanchipuram	Sriperumputhur	74	**Sri Eagambaraishwarar,** Sri Kailasanathar, Sri kachapeswarar
8	3.1. Chennai	3.1. Mamallapuram	Old OMR rd.	64	
9	3.2 Chennai	3.2 Kaveripakkam	Towards vellore and Bangalore	75	**Panchalinga iswar**
10	4. Mamallapuram	4. Thirukalukundram		10	**Vedagirishwarar**
11	4.1. Thirukalukundram	4.1. Chengalpattu		15	
12	4.2. Chengalpattu	4.2. Thirupulivanam	Via utramerur	45	**Viyakrapuriswar**
13	4.3. Chengalpattu	4.3. Vilupuram			
14	4.4. Vilupuram	4.4. Cuddalore			
15	4.5. Cuddalore	4.5. Chidambaram			
16	4.6. Chengalpattu	4.6. Kanchipuram		35	

TAMILNADU SHIVA TEMPLES TRAVEL GUIDE

	Origin Town	Temple town	Via	KM	Temples on the way (Brown one are 108 siva temples)
17	4.7. Kanchipuram	**4.7. Thiruvothore**	In Seyaru		**Vedapuriswar**
18	4.8. Seyaru	**4.8. Thiruvannamali**			
19	5. Kanchipuram	**5. Vellore.**		90	**Sri jalakandaeshwarar**
20	5.1. Vellore	**5.1. Virinchipuram**		19	In palar river bed built old siva temple.
21	5.2. Virinchipuram	**5.2. Vaniyambadi**		55	From vaniyambadi 5km in old vaniyambadi Siva temple
22	5.3. Vaniyambad	**5.3. Salem**			**Sugavaneshwar**
23	5.4. Salem	**5.4. Erode**			Thiruchengkodui-Arthanarishwarar
24	5.5 Erode	**5.5. Bhavani**		15	**Sangameshwarar**
25	5.6. Erode	**5.6. Coimbatore**			
26	5.7. Coimbatore	**5.7. Karur**	Palladam-Kangeyam		
27	5.8. Karur	**5.8. Thrichy**			
28	5.9. Vellore	**5.9. Odugathur**	Via Annaikattu	38	**Sabthariswar**
29	6. Vellore.	**6. Thiruvannamalai**		92	**Sri Arunachaleshwarar**
30	Thiruvanamalai	Sankarapuram	Kaduvanur		**Dhandeshwar**
31	6.1. Thiruvannamalai	**6.1. Thirukovilur**		32	**Verataeshwar**
32	6.2. Thirukovilur	**6.2. Paniyapuram**	From Vilupuram 10Km		**Panangkattu iswar**

TAMILNADU SHIVA TEMPLES TRAVEL GUIDE

	Origin Town	Temple town	Via	KM	Temples on the way (Brown one are 108 siva temples)
33	6.3. Vilupuram	6.3. Thiruvathigai	Banrooti		Verataneshwar
34	6.4. Banrooti	6.4. Thiruvakari	Towards Pandicheery		Chnadra mouliswar
35	7. Pandicheery	7. Cuddalore		25	
36	7.1. Banrooti	7.1. Thiruturiyur			Pasupathi iswar
37	7.2. Banrooti	7.2. Cuddalore			Sri Padaliswarar
38	7.3. Cuddalore	7.3. Virdachalam			
39	8. Villupuram	8. Virdachalam			
40	8.1. Thiruvannamalai	8.1. Virdachalam		94	Viruthagirishwarar
41	9. Virdachalam	9. Kombakonam	Gangaikonda cholapuram	48	Annaikari, Thirupananthal, Thiruvaipadi
42	9.1. Virdachalam	9.1. Chidambaram	Sri Muishnam	17	Natarajar
43	9.2. Chidambaram	9.2. Seerkalzi			Satanathar, umamaheshwarar &pramapuriswarar in three Sanctram in this temple.
44	9.3. Seerkalzi	9.3. Thirupariyalur	Myladudurai	35	Verataeshwar
45	9.4. Seerkazhi	9.4. Thiruvenkadu	Towards Poombokar	14	Swatharanyar(Thiruvenkadu)
46	9.5. Thiruvenkadu	9.5. Kizperumpallam (20km)	Via Poombokar	7	Naganathar
47	9.6. Thiruvenkadu	9.6. Thirukadaiyur	Via Poombokar and Towards Thirunalaru	23	

TAMILNADU SHIVA TEMPLES TRAVEL GUIDE

	Origin Town	Temple town	Via	KM	Temples on the way (Brown one are 108 siva temples)
48	9.7. Thirukadaiyur	9.7. Thirunalaru (53Km)	karikal	30	Shaniswar
49	9.8. Thirunalaru	9.8. Nagapattinam	Karaikal	28	Kaayaroganeshwar
50	9.9. Karaikal	9.9. Thirukarayal	Thirunatiyathan kudi		Kannayaranathar
51	10. Nagapattinam	10. Thiruvitkudi	Sikal, Sivalur, Nannilam near, Thiruvarur	22	Verataneshwar,
52	10.1. Nagapattinam	10.1. Thiruvayur	Ettukudi		Thiruvayuorenathan
53	10.2. Nagapattinam	10.2. Vedaraniyam	Velangkanni	57	
54	10.3. Nagapattinam	10.3. Thirumarikadu	Vedaraniyam	40	Vedavaneshwarar
55	10.4. Vedaraniyam	10.4. kachanam	Towards Thiruturaipoondi	20	Kachineshwar
56	10.5. kachanam	10.5. Thiruturaipoondi		5	Howsadiswar
57	10.6. Kachanam	10.6. Thiruvarur	Via Thiruturaipondi	20	Vanmiginathar
58	10.7. Thiruvarur	10.7. Nannilam	Poonthotaam	20	Thiruvizinathar
59	10.8. Poonthotaam	10.8. Sethalapathi	Towards Myladudurai	3	Mukthishwar
60	10.9. Nannilam	10.9. Thirukondiswaram		7	Pasupathi iswar
61	10.10. Nannilam	10.10. Thirusathamangai	Towards Nagapattinam		Ayavanthiswar
62	10.11. Nannilam	10.11. Kodavasal		20	
63	10.12. Kodavasal	10.12. Nachiyar koil		10	

TAMILNADU SHIVA TEMPLES TRAVEL GUIDE

	Origin Town	Temple town	Via	KM	Temples on the way (Brown one are are 108 siva temples)
64	10.13. Nachiyar koil	**10.13. Kombakonam**		10	
65	10.14. Kombakonam	**10.14. Sri vangiyam**	Towards nannilam	10	**Vangia lingaiswar**
66	11.0. Kombakonam	**11.0. Alangudi**		17	**Abathsaga iswar**
67	11.1. Alangudi	**11.1. Thiru Avalinallur**	Needamangalam	10	**Satchinathar**
68	11.2. Needamangalam	**11.2. Mannarkudi**		2	
69	11.3. Mannarkudi	**Kelzuvathur**	Towards muthupet		**Jadayupuriswar**
70	11.4. Thiruvarur	**11.4. Thanjaore**	Mannarkudi	60	Mannarkudi (30km), Alangudi (38)Ammapet, Saliamangalam (44km)
71	12. Seerkalzi	**12.0. Vaitheswaran koil**		16	**Vaithyanathar**, Sri Mullaivananatha swami
72	12.1. Vaitheswaran koil	**12.1. Kilzperumpallam**	Towards Poombookar		**Naganathar**
73	12.2. Vaitheswaran koil	**12.2. Myladudurai**		8	**Mayuranathar**, Thiruvadudurai-(komudeshwarar), Sayavanam-(Sri sayavaneshwarar), Sembanar koil- (sri Sornapurishwarar)
74	12.3. Vaitheswaran koil	**12.3. Thiruponkur**		3	Sivaloga nathar
75	12.4. Myladudurai	**12.4. Thiruvilanagar**	Towards thirukadaiyur	7	**Turaikattum vallalar**
76	12.5. Myladudurai	**12.5. Sembanar koil**	Towards thirukadaiyur	12	**Thiru Sempoonpalliyar**

TAMILNADU SHIVA TEMPLES TRAVEL GUIDE

	Origin Town	Temple town	Via	KM	Temples on the way (Brown one are 108 siva temples)
77	12.6. Myladudurai	**12.6. Thirukadaiyur**		22	Amirthakadeashwarar
78	12.7. Myladudurai	**12.7. Thiruvalzuore**		7	**Keerthivasan**
79	12.8. Myladudurai	**12.8. Thirukurkai**	Manalmedu		Yogeshwar
80	12.9. Myladudurai	**12.9. Thirumarukal**	Towards thiruvarur	20	**Manikavannar**
81	12.10. Myladudurai	**12.10. Keeranore**	Towards Thiruvarur	13	**Sivaloganathar**
82	12.11. Myladudurai	**12.11. Thirukodika**	Towards kutalam	7	**Koteshwar**
83	13. Myladudurai	**13. Kombakonam**	Adudurai	37	Sri Banapuriswarar
84	13.1. Kombakonam	**13.1. Suriyanar koil**		18	**Suriyanar Koil(18km),**
85	13.2. Suriyanar koil	**13.2. Kanjanur**		3	**Natarajar**
86	13.3. Kanjanur	**13.3. Thirumananjcheri**		6	**Utvaganathar**
87	13.4. Thirumananjcheri	**13.4. Kombakonam**	Adudurai	30	Kuthalam (5km), Adudurai (15km), Thiruvidaimaruthur (22km) Thirubhuvanam (24Km)
88	KOMBAKONAM NEAR TEMPLES				**Thirubhuvanam-Kambaeswar, Thiruvidaimaruthur-Sri Mahalingaswami, Thirunageshwaram-Naganathaswami, Dharasuram-Sri Jaravatheswarar, Pattishwaram-Pattishwarar, Thiruvalamsulzi. Abimugeshwarar, Kasi vishwanathar, Sri Someshwarar, Sri Somanathar, Sri Gouthameshwarar, Sri Kalahasthe iswarar, Sri Agambarashwarar**
89	Kombakonam	**Thirupananthaz**	Towards Anaikari	12	**Thadaneswar**

129

TAMILNADU SHIVA TEMPLES TRAVEL GUIDE

	Origin Town	Temple town	Via	KM	Temples on the way (Brown one are 108 siva temples)
90	Thirupananthaz	Thirumangalakudi		8	Prananatheswar
91	Kombakonm	S. Puthur	Towards thirunallaru	18	Sanathkumaraeswar
92	S. Puthur	Thirupampuram	Via Kolumangudi	10	Sesapuriswar
93	Kombakonm	Thiruvalzancholzhi	Towards Tanjore	6	Karpaganatha iswar
94	Kmobakonam	Thirukulam puthur	Towards south of kombakonam	20	Vilvanathar
95	Kombakonam	Bapanasam	Towards Tanjore	13	
96	Bapanasam	Thirukarukavur	Towards Tanjore	6	Chakravageswar
97	Bapanasam	Ayampettai	Towards Tanjore	13	Vasist iswar
98	Ayampettai	Thitai	Towards Tanjore	9	
99	14. Thitai	14. Thanjaore	thiruvidaimaruthur	13	108 lingams. (14Km from kombakonam). Pragadiswarar, Mullaivananathar (Thirukarkavur) Mahalingeswar (Thiruvidaimaruthur)
100	14.1. Thanjaore	14.1. Thirukandiyur	Thiruvayaru	17	Verataaneshwar
101	14.2 Thirukandiyur	14.2 Thiruvayaru		5	Iyyarapaan
102	14.3 Thiruvayaru	14.3 Thirupalaznam		4	Abathsaga ishwar
103	14.4 Thiruvayaru	14.4 Thirukuvalazi		19	Kolilinathar

TAMILNADU SHIVA TEMPLES TRAVEL GUIDE

	Origin Town	Temple town	Via	KM	Temples on the way (Brown one are 108 siva temples)
104	14.5 Thiruvayaru	**14.5 Thingalaru**		8	
105	14.6 Thiruvayaru	**14.6 Thiruchotruturi**	Kandiyur	10	**Chotruthurai iswar**
106	14.7 Thiruvayaru	**14.7 Thilai isthanam**		1.5	**Neyadiappar**
107	14.8 Thiruvayaru	**14.8 Thirumalzapadi**	Pulambadi railway station 15KM	17	**Vathiyanathan**
108	14. 9Kandiyur	**14.9 Thiruvedickudi**		3	**Vedapuri ishwar**
109	14. 10 Kandiyur	**14.10 Thiruponth thruthi**		3	**Pushpavaneshwar**
110	15 Thanjore	**15 Thirukadavur**	Mayuram-Thrangampadi		**Amirthakadeshwar**
111	15.1. Thanjaore	**15.1. Thingalaore**	. Thiruvayaru	25	Pancha Nadhiswarar in Thiruvayaru, **Thingaluru**(8Km from Thiruvayaru)
112	16. Kombakonam	**16. Thiruvayaru**	Thingalaru	32	Swamimalai(7km), **Thingaluru**(38km)
113	16.2. Kombakonam	**16.2. Andangkoil**	valangaiamman and Kudavasal	10	**Swarnapuri iswar**
114	16.1. Thiruvayaru	**16.1. Pazaore**	Keelapazaore	17	**Vadamulanathar**
115	Keelapazaore	**Lalkudi**	Towards thrichy	17	**Sabthariswar**
116	16.2 Lalkudi	**16.2. Thiruverumbur**		13	**Erumbeshwar**

TAMILNADU SHIVA TEMPLES TRAVEL GUIDE

	Origin Town	Temple town	Via	KM	Temples on the way (Brown one are 108 siva temples)
117	16.3. Thiruverumbur	**16.3. Thiruvanikaval**		05	**Sri Jambugeswarar**
118	16.4. Thiruvanikaval	**16.4. Thrichy**	Chatiram bus Stand	07	**Thayumanavar** –Located In hill top.
119	17.1. Thrichy	**17.1. Uraiyur**	Chatiram bus Stand		Sri Pancha varneshwarar
120	17.2. Thrichy	**17.2. Payanjili**		20	Sri Nelakandeshwar
121	17.3. Thrichy	**17.3. Thiru Pattur**		30	Sri Brama puriswarar
122	17.4 Thrichy	**17.4 Nedungudi**	Aranthagi and Karaikudi		**Kailasanathar**
123	17.5. Thrichy	**17.5. Thirunedungkalam**	Tuvakudi	7	**Nithya sundarar**
124	17.6 Thrichy	**17.6. Karur**		76	Psupathiswarar
125	18. Karur	**18. Erode**		64	**Aruthra Kabalishwar**
126	18.1. Erode	**18.1. Thiruchengkodu**		18	Sri Arthanarishwarar
127	18.2. Erode	**18.2. Bhavani**		14	**Sri Sangameshwarar**
128	18.3. Erode	**18.3. Namakal**			
129	19. Erode	**19. Coimbatore**			Velangiri hills(30km), Dhiyanalingam(30km)
130	19.1. Coimbatore	**19.1. 10Km From Madathukulam**	Inbetween Udumali-Palani Route		**Archuneswar**

TAMILNADU SHIVA TEMPLES TRAVEL GUIDE

	Origin Town	Temple town	Via	KM	Temples on the way
					(Brown one are 108 siva temples)
131	20. Coimbatore	20. Madurai	Palani-Tindukal		Palani, Meenakshi temple (3600 years old), Kodal alagar perumal, Alagar koil, Thiruparang kundram, Palamuthircholai
132	20.1 Coimbatore	20.1 Perur		5	**Patteshwar**
133	21. Thrichy	21. Madurai		162	Thiruwapudiyar, Thiruwadavur-Thirumarainathar(26km), Thiruvedakam-Adaganathar
134	21.1. Madurai	21.1. Karaikudi	Pillayarpatti	120	Kundrakudi(10km), Pillayarpatti ganesh(13km)
135	21.2. Pillayarpatti	21.2. Thirupattur	Sivagangai route	7	Sri Thiruthalinganathar koil here **(Midnight pooja)** carried out daily
136	21.3. Thirupattur	21.3. Ahavudayar koil	Sirar Perumdurai	35	**Atmanathar**
137	21.4. Ahavudayar koil	21.4. Thiruvadanai		35	**Adirataneswar**
138	21.5. Thiruvadanai	21.5Ramanathapuram		100	
139	21.6. Ramanathapuram	21.6. Rameshwaram		30	**Ramanathaswami koil,** Kothandaramaswami
140	21.7. Ramanathapuram	21.7. Utrakosamangai		18	**Mangalanathar**

TAMILNADU SHIVA TEMPLES TRAVEL GUIDE

	Origin Town	Temple town	Via	KM	Temples on the way (Brown one are 108 siva temples)
141	21.8. Ramanathapuram	21.8. Thirupulani		14	
142	21.9. Thirupulani	21.9. Tuticorin	Sikal-salkudi		
143	22.0 Ramanathapuram	22. Madurai		150	Sundaresar
144	22.1 Madurai	22.1.	In Thenkasi route	70	
145	22.2. Srivilliputur	Srivilliputur 22.2. Sankaran koil		48	Sankarankoil(combine of siva &vishnu statue) Audi Tapus festival famous
146	22.3. Sankaran koil	22.3. Thirunelvelli		45	Gandhimathi Nellaiappar(Built 700 CE)
147	22.4. Thirunelvelli	22.4. Krishnapuram		30	Krishnapuram perumal(Good sculpture)
148	22.5. Thirunelvelli	22.5. Thenkasi		55	
149	22.6. Thenkasi	22.6. Papanasam			Papanasa nathar
150	22.7. Papanasam	22.7. Cheran mahadevi		15	Ammanatha swami
151	22.8 Cheran mahadevi	22.8 Kodakanallur	Nadukallur and Muk kudal		Kailasanathar

TAMILNADU SHIVA TEMPLES TRAVEL GUIDE

	Origin Town	Temple town	Via	KM	Temples on the way (Brown one are 108 siva temples)
152	22.9. Cheran mahadevi	**22.9. Thirunelvelli**		30	
153	22.10 Thirunelveli	**22.10 Kunnathur**	Mela thiruvenkata nathapuram		**Kothaparameshwar**
154	22.11 Thirunelveli	**22.11 Chertha Poomangalam**	Towards Punnaikayal route		**Kailasanathar**
155	22.12 Thirunelveli	**22.12 Murappu Nadu**	To wards Tuticorin	17	**Kailasanathar**
156	22.13. Thirunelvelli	**22.13. Sri Vaikondam**	To wards Thiruchendur	30	**Kailasanathar**
157	22.14 Sri Vaikondam	**22.14 Thiruchendur**		32	Thiruchendur muruga
158	22.15. Sir Vaikondam	**22.15. Rajapathi**		8	**Kailasanathar**
159	22.16 Rajapathi	**22.16 Thenthiruperai**	Thenthiruperai	8	**Sri kailasanthar**
160	22.17. Thenthiruperai	**22.17. Tuticorin`**	Manathi	35	
161	23. Thiruchendur	**23. Tuticorin**		62	
162	24. Madurai	**24. Tuticorin**	Ettayapuram	133	Kovilpati Ganesh temple
163	24.1 Tuticorin	**24.1 Sri Vaikondam**	Navathirupathi(All temples within 10km)	30	Vaikondam, Thiruvaragunamangai, Thirupuliyamkodi; Twin thirupathi, Perungkulam, Thentiruporai, Thirukolur, Alwar Thirunagri.

TAMILNADU SHIVA TEMPLES TRAVEL GUIDE

	Origin Town	Temple town	Via	KM	Temples on the way (Brown one are 108 siva temples)
164	24.2. Sri Vaikondam	24.2. Thirunelvelli		30	Neliyapar temple
165	24.3. Thirunelvelli	24.3. Papanasam		60	
166	24.4. Thirunelvelli	24.4. Nanguneri	Kaniyakumari route	29	Vanamaamalai perumal with 10 Suanbu murty famous one.
167	24.5. Nanguneri	24.5. Thirkurungkudi		12	For Siva and Biravar statue provided
168	24.6. Nanguneri	24.6. Kaniyakumari		62	Kumari amman temple. Gurunatheswarar
169	24.7. Kaniyakumari	24.7. Susinthiram		14	Sri isthanu maalayan koil.(Statue is combine of Siva, Vishnu & Brama)
170	24.8. Susinthiram	24.8. Nagarkoil		5	Nagaraja temple.
171	24.9. Nagarkoil	24.9. Thiruvataru	Alzagiya mandapam	40	
172	24.10. Thiruvataru	24.10. Tiruvandram			
173	25. Thirunelvelli	25. Papanasam	Ambasamudiram	60	Papavinasar koil
174	25.1. Papanasam	25.1. Nagerkoil	Cheranmaha devi	75	
175	25.2. Nagerkoil	25.2. Therisanangkupu		12	Ragaveshwar
176	25.3. Nagerkoil	25.3. Susinthiram		5	Dhanu
177	25.4. Marthandam	25.4. Thirunandhikarai		13	Nandhiswar
178	25.5. Susinthiram	25.5. Nagerkoil		5	

NAVAGRAGHA ISTHLANGAL IN AND AROUND KUMBOKONAM

1. Suriyanor koil- (Suriyan isthalam)
2. Thingaluru-(Chandrian isthalam).
3. Alangudi-(Guru isthalam)
4. Thirunageshwaram-(Ragu isthalam)
5. Thiruvenkadu-(Puthan)
6. Kanjanur-(Sukran)
7. Kizperumpallam-(Kethu isthalam)
8. Thirunallaru-(Shani isthalam)
9. Vaitheeswaran koil-(Sevai isthalam).

From Kombakonam about 35Km thanjore the great temple is thre you can visit and enjoy the sculupture work of this temple.

TANJORE GREAT PRAGATHESWARAR TEMPLE

NAVAGRAGHA ISTHLANGAL ROAD MAP

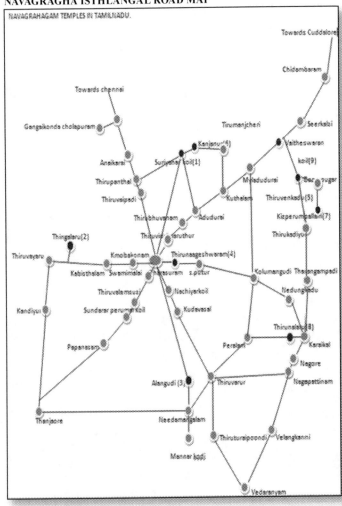

NAVAGRAHAGAM TEMPLES IN TAMILNADU.

Navathirupathi temple:

The Nava thirupathi temple can be approached either from Tuticorin(36 Km) or Thirunelvelli (28Km). The train/bus facility available to Sri Vaikondam from above mentioned cities bus frequency is more. These Nava thirupathi temples reference were taken from the Nam Alwar Mangalasasanam poems. These temples are located at a peripheral distance of 44 Km. on the river tamirabharani both the banks aside. For seeing all the temple 5 to 7 Hrs Needed in normal condition. The Auto facility available at nominal from Sri Vaikondam they ask for Rs. 550 to 600 to show all the temples.

The temple and God names mentioned in the table.				
Place Name	Temple Name	God name	God's Posture	Associated Gragha
Sri Vaikondam	Kazhapiran	Sri Vaikondanathan	Standing	Suriyan(Sun)
Varagunamangai-Natham	Vijayasanap Perumal	Vijasana paramapatha nathan	Sitting	Chandiran (Moon)
Thirupuliyangkudi	Kaaichinanvenda perumal	Sri Boomibalagar	Laying	Puthan
Tholavillimangalam	Eratti thirupathi	Sri Arvinda lotchana perumal	Sitting	Kethu
Tholavillimangalam	Eratti thirupathi	Sri Devarpiran	Standing	Ragu
Perumkulam	Thirukulaznthai	Mayakuthar	Standing	Saniswarar
Thentirupperai	Thenthirupperai	Magara Nedun kuzhaikaathar	Sitting	Sukran
Thirukkolloor	Vaithamanidhi	Vaithamanidhi. madura kavi alwar	Laying	Sevvai
Alwarthirunagari	Adinathaalwar	Adinathar. Namalwar	Standing	Viyazhan

KANCHIPURAM HISTORY:

It is 76 Km from Chennai. It is capital town during Pallva's regime. It is rich in heritage by accompany lot of temples within it hence it is also called as temple town of tamilnadu. It is one among seven Motcha isthalm in india. Among 208 Divaya desam in india it itself have 14 Divya desam.

In 1958 this district formed as Chengai MGR dt. then named as Chengai anna dt. and in tradition is called as Kanchipuram now. In 1996 this kanchi Dt is dived into as Thirvaluvar and present Kanchipuram dt.

As per 2001 sensex this Dt is grown very fast in population, present days the Rapid Development happening due to its industrial hub. The most of the car industries located here. It is having SEZ zone and may turn into ASIA's biggest industrial park. It is famous for lot of lakes(3696) within it now days these lakes become residential and industrial complex this has to be taken for preserving water resource we have.

Kancheepuram famous for handloom silk saris world wide. The sari cost starts from Rs.1000 onwards and end up in lacks. In Tamilnadu it is pride to have costliest silk sari in their family.

KANCHIPURA	DISTRICT	TEMPLES		
Mamallapuram Thirukalzukundram Vallak kottai Melmaruvathur Kumara Kumara kuttam Adiparasakthi				
DIVYA DESAM TEMPLES IN KANCHIPURAM DISTRICT				
Thiruputkolzi, Thirukachi, stapuyagaram, Thiruthaniga, Thiruvelukai, Thiruneeragam, Thiruorugam, Thirupadakam, Thirunilla thingal thondam, Thiruvetka, Thirukaragam, Thirukarvanam, Thirukalvanar, Thirupavala vannam, Thiruparameshwara vinnagaram.				
KANCHI TEMPLES				
Kachabeshwarar Vaikonda perumal kamatchi Amman Ulakalantha perumal Kailasanathar				
Agambareshwarar Panda thuthar Thropathi amman				
DIVIYA DESAM TEMPLES IN KANCHIPURAM				
1. Sri Adi varada perumal inside kamatchi amman temple 2. Inside Ulagalantha peruma temple four divya desam are there(A. Thiru ooragam B. Thiru Neeragam C. Thiru Karagam D. Thiru Kaarvaanam) 3. Thiruparameshwara vinnagaram inside Vaikonda perumal temple 4. Thirunilla thingal thondam temple inside Egambareshwarar temple 5. Thirupavala vannam 6. Sri Pachai vannam				
OLD KANCHIPURAM DIVYA DESAM				
7. Thirukachi inside the Varada raja perumal temple. 8. Thiruvetka inside Yothogarai peruma temple 9. Thiruvelukai inside the Azaghia singar perumal temple 10. Thiruthaniga inside Vilakoli perumal temple 11. Thiruputkolzi inside vijaya ragava perumal temple				

MAMALAPURAM TEMPLE:

It has got world heritage sea temple on sea shore present day only one temple available remaining six temples sunk in the sea. In recent sunami happened in india that time some of the temples start visible during low tide period.

It has got Pancha Rath made up of monolithic stones.

It has got olden perumal temple where the diety in laid down condition and near by to this temple you can find arjun penance caves.

On hill top you can find light house and maa ka cave temples.

From here the thirukaluzk kundram just 12 km try to visit this temple in forenoon time, here the two eagles coming daily for taking Prasad of lord iswar more than many decades.

It is olden days port during pallva kingdoms the inscription shows during that period the east asian countries had trade through this port, now days it become famous tourism sport of tamilnadu.

Lot of cottage type lodges available too stay here peacefully.

END OF CHAPTER-4

Chapter 5

KARNATAKA TEMPLES

BADAMI AND ITS NEARBY TEMPLES.

It is the capital of early chalukya Dynasty in the period of 543 to 566 CE. It is located in Bagalkot dt. of northern Karnataka. From Bagalkot by road good connectivity is there.

Bhagalkot-Badami (36km), Badami-Bhansankari amman temple(05Km), Bhansankari temple - Pattadakal(20Km), Pattadakal-Aihole(12Km), Aihole-Amingad(9km), Amingad-Kudala Sangama(12km) where you can see the Kudala sangameshwarar temple. Kudala sangama- Almatti(30Km), Almatti-Bijapur(60km).

From hosepet via Gadag train/bus facilty available to Badami(169 km). From hubli 108km to Badami

It has got North and south forts on hill top and many temples in these forts. These temples were made up of fusion of North and South Indian temples styles.

In Northern side hill top

1. Malrgitti Sivalaya.
2. Upper Sivalaya and
3. Lower of the hill lower Sivalaya.

4. Bhutanatha temple
5. Hanuman temple.

In Southern hill there are 4 caves and fort made in hill top. From Gadag to hosepet going road you can find lot of windmill in outer skirts of Gadag. In Gadag near new bus stand Buswana statue very big in size you can find approx. 60ft. high.

VIJAYANAGAR DYNASTY TEMPLES.

The vijayanagar dynasty existed from 1336 AC to 1680 AC. Sangama dynasty ruled from 1336 to 1486. Salva dynasty 1486 to 1503. Tulu dynasty 1503 to 1569. Aravidu dynasty 1572 to 1680 ruled this kingdom.

In this Krishna devaraya in tulu dynasty is remarkable king during his period the kingdom flourished in central decan india, its capital was Hampi located in southern banks of Tungabatra river near present Hosepet. It is located around 130 Km from Guntakal (located in Chennai to Mumbai train route) and 67 from Bellary. From hyderbad, Bangalore, thirupati and Miraj trains facility available to Hosepet. Hampi is 12 km from hosepet. One must spend full day to enjoy and peacefully see the all the ruined temples over here. It has got Several temples they are

1. Virupaksha temple it has got 165 ft high tower at the entrance(it is called as Hampi main tower).
2. Veerabhuvaneswara temple in Matunga hill.
3. Kodanda Rama temple.
4. Vittala temple.(World famous stone charot is there in this temple)
5. Achyutaraya temple.
6. Purandara Mantapa
7. kings balance.
8. Vijaya vittala temple
9. Kadalekalu Ganapathi 18ft high monolithic ganapathi is there here.
10. Krishna temple

11. Badavi linga.
12. Ugra Narasimha.
13. Pataleswara temple
14. Sister's rock
15. Hajara Rama temple.
16. Mahanavami dibba.
17. Lotus mahal.
18. Hemakutta Jain temple.
19. Elephant stable.
20. Queen's bath.
21. Malyavantha Raghunatha temple.
22. Pushkarani.
23. Kamalapur Musuem
24. Malikarjuna temple.
25. Anantashayana Gudi
26. Tungabhadra Dam

Apart from this south Karnataka Saravana belagula jain statue, Udupi Krishna temple, Dharam isthala, and Mysore samundiswari temple and mysore dasra festival carried out in mysore palace you must see.

BADAMI LORD BHUTANATHA TEMPLE

WORLD FAMOUS STONE CHARIOT IN VITAL TEMPLE

Chapter 6

ANDHRA PRADESH TEMPLES

VIJAYAWADA TEMPLES.

From Chennai 431 Km the vijayawada is located. From Chennai to kolkutta railway or bus route we can find vijayawada.

Kanaka Durga Devi temples:

It is located in Vijayawada town itself on hill top. Krishna reservoir dam and entire view of city makes more excitation and marvelous panoramic view from temple. In the month of July lot of devotees comes to this temple it is consider auspicious month to visit this temple. The Dasara festival is famous too here. Form Vijayawada railway station just 02 km to the temple. To claim this temple steps has been provided and APSRTC bus service too available up to hill top.

Mangalagiri temples

From Vijayawada 12 km to the Mangalagiri just opposite to bus stand the road proceed to Mangalagiri BANAKALU

Narasimar temple, Just 1km from Mangalagiri bus stand. The Steps were provided to reach hill top and share auto facility too available to take you to the temple and back they ask Rs30 only per person. The Speciality of Banakalu Narasimar is whatever water puts on his mouth he just takes inside nobody knows where this water goes till now. People offer water to this Narasimar as offering, the temple Garpagirah is very small and moorthy also too small.

After visitng narasimar if go for Sikkara Darshan you can find entire Mangalagiri Panoromic view with Sikkara Darsan. In the caves the Nagaraja idols were there. Adjacent to that you can find The Vishnu in laying position. This temple is one of the famous nine temple of Narasimar in the Andhra Pradesh. The other famous Narasimar temples are in AP are.

2. Ahobelam 3. Pendhala kone 4. Yadagiri gutta 5. Ander vedi 6. Shimachalam in visakapattinam 7. Vedaathri 8. Polengar and 9. Dharmapuri

RAJARAJESWARI TEMPLE:

On the way to the Mangalagiri hill top temple you can find Sri Rajarajeswari temple with Jayanjatic entrance Gopuram welcomes you have Maaka Darsan there.

AMARAVATHI TEMPLES:

From Vijayawada or Guntur 34 km to the Amravati town located within walk able distance the Pancha rama temple is there. The God name is Amaralingeswarar. The temple is located at the banks of Krishna River. The devotees take bath in Krishna River and then proceed to the temple. The joy boat trip too available nearby temple to go to the opposite end of Krishna River banks.

BUDHA STUPA:

Amravati in olden days this was main town for Mahayana Buddhist. Here on the top of the Buddha ashes (Asti) the largest Stupa was built. It was 100 ft height and 138 ft. on Dia. With marvelous sculpture work and sayings of Buddha was encrypted on the structure stones. This is larger than Sanchi Stupi and built in BC 2ⁿᵈ century. Now days the ruins removed from stupa was displayed in the Museum. This Museum has been maintained by Archeology department one of the Indian destroyed monument.

PANCHARAMA TEMPLE:

The Pancha Rama temples located in Andra Pradesh in Krishna and Godavari districts.

1. Amaralingeshwarar in Amaravati in Guntur Dt. From Guntur 34 Km.(Devendiran installed and prayed this lingam)
2. Someshwaran in Bhimavaram of West Godavari dt. of AP(The Chandra installed and Prayed this lingam).
3. Sri Ramalingeshwarar in Palakulu in West Godavari Dt. of AP(The Rama installed and prayed this lingam) from Bimavaram 22 Km.
4. Kumara Bimaeshwaran (Goddess-Sri Balatiripura Sundari) in Samalkot in East Godavari Dt. of AP(Lord Subramaniyam installed and prayed this lingam) from Railway station 0.5Km.
5. Sri Bimeshwarar in Draksha Ram in AP.(The Sun installed and Prayed this lingam) from Kakinada 25km.

It is believed Lord Siva had lived in these places. The Pancha Rama temple history as follows. The Demon Dharakasuran strong devotee of Lord Siva. When Devodas and Demons grind the Milk sea for getting Amurtham out of it during this course of time Atma linga also came out. The Dharakasuran took This Atma linga and worn in his neck and prayed towards Ishwar and got the Boon of Ever living, on one condition that until he will not fight with HIM or HIS generation he will be living in this world. Due to this boon he has got enormous power he smash the devodas and made their life miserable. The affected Devodas request Lord Visnu to save them from this Demon.

The Lord Vishnu took all of them to Lord Siva explain the condition, lord Siva took their concern and revealed even though he is my devotee if he not follow Darma he has to be punished. My son Subramanian will smash him and take care all of you. The Lord Subramaniyam fought with Dharakasuran he could not able to kill him until he breaks the Atma lingam in his neck. This brocken Atma Linga fall in above mentioned 05 places. The broken Atma lingam tend to grow by virtue, hence wherever it fallen that place the Linga has to be installed firmly and regular poojas to be made inorder to avoid Growth to this Atma Linga pieces. Wherever this Atma linga pieces fallen, their this Pancha Rama temples were built.

SIMACHALAM TEMPLE IN VIZAG

Vishnu temple.

1. Thirupathi

END OF CHAPTER-6

Chapter 7

GUJARAT TEMPLES

JAMNAGAR TEMPLE.

Jain Temple

The Jain temple built in white marble is dedicated to Adinath the first tirthankara or apostle of Jains. The temple is decorated with paintings depicting incidents from the life of Tirthankaras. The first floor of the temple is particularly dedicated to Parasnath. His image has been carved out in black marble and images of planets adorn the ceiling as given in the Hindu mythology. There are 05 Jain temples here in Chandi Bazar of Jamnagar there were shown below. Inside this temple the 72 the jain gurus small shrines were. It has been told the Adinath is first Guru and Mahaveer is last Guru of Jains. 1. Pasvanath temple.

At this temple entrance you can find Devi-Chakeshwari and Devi Mariputhuru. 2. Choriwala temple 3. Shanthinath temple. 4. Bala Anuman Mandir. 5. Mahadev temple. Apart from above temple the most the jain temples in Junagard from Jamnagar 3 to 4 Hrs by road approx 180Km from Jamnagar. They are 1. Datatri jain temple. 2. Gowrinath Parvath 3. Ambaji

Mandir. 4. Lot of Jain temples. Here near by only the lion Sanactuary Gir forest too available. From Junagard 1.5 hrs drive to Somnath where you can find Somnath jothirlingam, Gita Mandir, Balukatheer and Krishna Samadhi and Thiruveni sangamam you can see.

Bala Anuman Mandir.

In this temple 24 hrs Bajan's going on without stop since 01.08.1964 till now. It had made Gunnes book record in this regard. Here Ram main mandir adjacent to the temple you can find lord siva. The temple was founded and maintained by Guruji you can find his samadhi(Prem phisuk maharaj) in the temple premises.

JAIN TEMPLE NEAR AKSHAIDAM TEMPLE MADE WITH MODERN ARCHITECT.

AHEMADABAD TEMPLES:

Akshaidam Swami narayana temple and adjacent Jain temple in Ahmedabad. Bholonath temple in River Sabarmati bed in Ahemdabad and Lord ganesha temple in Outerskirt Ahemadabad.

Krishna and Rukmani temple in Duwaraka. Pet duwaraka Krishna temple

Somnath temple in veravel.

SURAT:

Maataji temple and swamy narayana temple in Bhuruch and ankeleshear shiva temple.

END OF CHAPETR-7

Chapter 8

MADYAPRDESH TEMPLES

It has got Two famous jothilingam Omkareshwar and Mahakal temple just 75Km from Indore. Temples in Madhya Pradesh are very famous by virtue of their historical prominence. The Khajuraho temple for instance in Madhya Pradesh is so famous that people from different parts of the world visit this temple at least once in their life time to get enthralled by the very ancient erotic sculptures found on its walls. Among many Temples in Madhya Pradesh, the Sun Temple Madhya Pradesh, Kalbhairav Temple, Laxmi Narayan Temple, Kamadgiri Temple and Gopal Mandir are the famous Hindu temples in Madhya Pradesh and draw many devotees from India.

Khajuraho temples are the famous temples in Madhya Pradesh, which are scenically located in midst of forest at Bundelkhand and are recognized as the World Heritage Center. Every year from the 25th of February till 2nd of March, the Khajuraho temple comes alive with a brilliant display of Indian Classical Dance Festival, from famous artistes across the world.

The Sun Temple Madhya Pradesh also known as the Brahmanya Dev (Baramju) temple located at Unao, located at about 18 kilometers from Jhansi (UP) is also among the famous temples in Madhya Pradesh and rumors say that even the blind, lepers and many people with many other skin ailments are cured on visiting this shrine, which is dedicated to the Sun God. Sunday is considered to be the holy day and the day of special worship.

Joining the temples in Madhya Pradesh, the tombs also come alive with festive moments. In fond remembrance of the Tansen, the father of Hindustani Classical Music, his tomb at Guwalior town is reverberated with Hindustani Classical Music every year during the months of November and December, when the Annual Indian Classical Festival is held for five captivating night-long sessions, where the most notable and famous singers perform with abiding gusto all through the night.

The Narmada Udgam Temple, believed to be located at the source of the river Narmada in Amarantak is the one of the famous Hindu Temples in Madhya Pradesh and a famous pilgrimage destination also.

Kamadgiri Temple, located in the town of Chitrakoot has become famous as the temple of wishes—people believe that their wishes come true if they visit this temple. This beautiful is one of the famous temples in Madhya Pradesh and is located on the banks of the serene Mandakini River, amidst exquisite Vindhya Hills.

GWALIOR

Teli Ka Mandir.

This temple is an Architecture splendor which is located in Guwalior. This is the tallest and most impressive temple within the precincts of the Guwalior Fort. This particular Rajput Temple is an amalgam of the northern and southern architectural styles of India, although many opine that it is closer in design to the temples of Orissa than the South.

WAY TO THE TEMPLE

Through Air - Guwalior has an airport that is situated nearly just 8 km away from the heart of the city. The city of Guwalior is well connected by direct flights with all the major cities in India like - Delhi, Agra, Indore, Bhopal, Mumbai, Jaipur and Varanasi.

Through Road- there is a good road network connecting all the major places of Madhya Pradesh as well as other places of India with Guwalior. Guwalior city is well linked with by road ways include Agra, Jaipur, Delhi, Lucknow, Bhopal, Chanderi, Indore, Jhansi, Khajuraho, Ujjain, and Shivpuri.

Through Rail- the railway station in Guwalior is located on the Delhi-Mumbai and Delhi -Chennai rail track. The Railway transportation here also connects Guwalior with many other major cities of India.

Significance of the temple According to one of the legends, Rashtrakuta Govinda III occupied the Fort in 1794, and appointed the Telanga Brahmins to supervise all religious ceremonies. The temple got its name from them. According to another version of belief the monument is called the Teli Temple, because the men of Teli caste or oil merchants handled its construction. A third conjecture about the temple is that the name suggests a link with the Telangana region in modern Andhra Pradesh, which suggests the fusion of Dravidian and North Indian architectural styles.

Whatever the truth, the fact remains that the Teli Temple, is a marvellous amalgam of the architecture features of the temples of North and South India. The shikhara or a spire is definitely Dravidian in style, while the decorative details are in the Nagara style – specific to North India. Figures of river goddesses, amorous couples, coiled serpents, and a flying Garuda (Lord Vishnu's vehicle) abound in the temple complex.

Teli Ka Mandir is a very ancient temple that is undoubtedly famous for its splendid architecture. Located in the Guwalior Fort complex, Teli Ka Mandir can be reached easily by taking local means of transport from Guwalior. The English version of Teli Ka Mandir is Oilman's Temple. Built in 11th century, Oilman's Temple is the oldest temple of the Gwalior Fort.

Elevating to the height of 100 feet, Teli Ka Mandir is the tallest and most stunning temple in the confines of the Gwalior Fort. The temple is actually dedicated to Lord Vishnu in the form of his mount, Garuda. The colossal image of 'Garuda' (Mount of Lord Vishnu) is the major attraction of Teli Ka Mandir. This unusual image makes the circlet of the doorway, the highest structure in the Gwalior Fort.

KHAJURAHO TEMPLE

The City of Khajuraho is situated in the forested plains of Madhya Pradesh in the region known as Bundelkhand and at a reasonable distance from most cities and town centers of the state Main Attractions:Western Group of Temples, Eastern Group of Temples Southern Group of Temples Khajuraho Dance Festival: Khajuraho Dance Festival is held from – 25th Feb – 30th Feb World Heritage Site:

Right through the Mughal invasion and the early British forays into the country, Khajuraho temples in India remained unknown. Rediscovered in this century, they are fine reminders of India's glorious past.

Khajuraho Temples - Temples of Love

To some, Khajuraho Temples are the most graphic, erotic and a sensuous sculpture of India, the world has ever known. But Khajuraho has not received the attention it deserves for its significant contribution to the religious art of India – there are literally hundreds of exquisite images on the interior and exterior walls of the shrines.

Khajuraho Temples architecture

Architecturally these temples are unique. While each temple in Khajuraho has a distinct plan and design, several features are common to all. They are all built on high platforms, several metres off the ground, either in granite or a combination of light sandstone and granite. Each of these temples has an entrance hall or mandapa, and a sanctum sanctorum (main sanctum) or garbha griha. The roofs of these various sections have a distinct form. The porch and hall have pyramidal roofs made of several horizontal layers. The inner sanctum's roof is a conical tower - a colossal pile of stone (30m high) made of an arrangement of miniature towers called shikharas.

The famous Western groups of temples are designated as a World Heritage Site and are enclosed within a beautifully laid out park. The Lakshmana and Vishwanath Temples to the front and The Kandariya Mahadev, Jagadami and Chitragupta Temples displays the best craftmanship of Khajuraho

Khajuraho Temples complex

For the purpose of convenience, the village of Khajuraho has been divided into three directional areas where the major groups of temple complex are located. These are

Western Group Temples- These groups of Khajuraho temples are entirely Hindu, and constitute some of the finest examples of Chandela art at its peak. The largest being the Kandariya Mahadev temple, followed by a granite temple - Chaunsath Yogini. The Chitragupta Temple is dedicated to the Sun God, while the Vishwanath Temple sports a three-headed image of Brahma – the Creator of the Universe. The Lakshmana Temple is superbly decorated, while the Devi Jagdambi Temple is dedicated to Goddess Kali. Other temples in the Western Group include the Varaha Temple with a nine-foot high boar-incarnation of Lord Vishnu, the Matangeshwara Temple with a eight-feet high lingam, and the Brahma Temple.

Eastern Group Temples- This group of Khajuraho temples comprises of two historic Jain temples. The Adinath Temple lavishly embellished with sculpted figures, and the Parsvanath Temple which is the largest Jain temple, sculpted with charming detail. There are other shrines such as the Vamana Temple with apsaras (fairies) in sensuous poses, and the Javari Temple that has a richly-carved doorway.

Southern Group Temples- This southern group has two impressive temples, mainly belonging to the 12th century – the Chaturbhuj Temple, with a massive, carved image of Vishnu, and the Duladeo Temple, one of the last temples of the Chandela era, dedicated to Lord Shiva. Symbolizing a medieval legacy, the Khajuraho temples of India are a perfect combination of architectural and sculptural excellence, representing one of the finest examples of Indian art.

Shopping And Souvenirs Around Khajuraho Temples- Being one of the most visited temples in India, many shops have mushroomed around the temple complex which offers souvenirs at best of prices. There are number of stalls in front of these temples that present a wide array of articles which are worth buying.

Khajuraho Temple Dance Festival- This dance festival is held every year from 25th February to 2nd March, the Khajuraho Dance festival has become a platform that showcase some of the best and distinctive Indian classical dance forms that include Bharatnatyam, Kathak, Odisi, Kathakali etc. For over 25 years now, the carved stones fill with life during the month of Feb as music and dance take centers stage as in the former days.

How to Reach Khajuraho Temples

Air- The airport is 5 kms from the city centre and is well connected by domestic flights to and from Agra, Varanasi and Kathmandu.

Train- Mahoba, Satna and Jhansi are the nearest railway stations. All of these are well connected by most of the major cities of India.

Road- Khajuraho is connected by regular bus services with Mahoba, Harpalpur, Satna, Jhansi, Gwalior, Agra, Jabalpur and Bhopal. Khajuraho is 590 kms from Delhi via Gwalior and Jhansi.

INDORE TEMPLES.

Indore is 190 Km from Bhopal. Both the place have domestic well connected by Air, train and bus facility. The indore region was ruled by queen Ahilyabai, she had made more temple construction and renovation activities during her ruling period.

Indore has got three modern art temples.

1. Annapurana temple
2. Gaaz(Class) Mehal in cloth market area
3. Gajarana Ganapathy temple.

1. Annapurana temple.

In this temple For lord Siva, Lord Vishnu, Lord Krishna and Anjaneyar separate shrines were there.

Annapurana devi main shrine is built. The temple Garpagirah and its adjacent wall were depicted with Purana description of events in sculpture work made by cement and special material called sothai. Nice to see the the entrance Gopura and 04 Gigantic elephant made in sculpture at the temple entrance.

2. Gaaz Mehal.

This Jain temple located in cloth market in busiest place of Indore.

The temple outside looks like house only, if you go inside and see the walls and roofs were marvellously decorated with different coloured Glass piececs. I can't descripe you must see and enjoy this typical jain temple. This temple has been built and maintained by jain family, they sells CD of the temple construction and view of the entire temple in CD you Can by and get the details of this temple, Inside the temple Photography not allowed.

Gajarana Ganapathy temple.

It is modern art temple comprise main shine for Ganesha, apart from that several other Devi and God's Lot shrines were there which includes underground Sivashine too. Nice temple see and enjoy in your own. Visiting at evening time you can enjoy and get pleasure in this temple by virtue of its environment.

BHOPAL TEMPLES

Bhopal is approx 500Km from Delhi and 600 Km from jaipur, this Madya Pradesh capital is connected by air and train facility from renowned Metro cities of india.

It has got following famous temple in this region.

1. Gopa Mandir in Hill top

This temple is easily approachable, located in Midest of old Bhopal. The temple utilized caves portion for constructing Lord Krishna shrine here. The caves which was formed naturally seems to go endless, where the human has to cravel and go inside this caves. At the entrance of these caves lord Siva shrine were there. People making special offering to Lord Siva with local Pandit available here. These temple complex have accommodation for Pandit in and Bramacharis in temple premises itself. There are approx 100 steps are there to reach top of this temple. Upon reaching temple Panoromic view of old Bhopal you can enjoy

2. Nandeshwara Jain temple

Just opposite to Gopa Mandir this Jain temple is there walk able distance only. This jain temple typical in it s nature of construction. The main Shrine in located in Dome shape Garpagirah. In this 4 Segments in circular shape made. In each segment 13 Jain prophet statue were there, like that in total 4 segments you can see total 52 Prophet of jains you can find. The devotees sit in an arc shape rows and make Jabaas by offering rice to this prophet.

3. Aadinath Jain temple at Hill top.

This temple 1 km from Gopa Mandir, at a foot hill you can find cable car facility too available to reach this temple. Marveouls experience you can have during your visit, lets try. This temple is Night time illuminated with lights from far distance you can see this entire temple view. From Bhopal airport also this temple view you can find.

4. Birla Mandir

It is located in New Bhopal near by Rastria Bhavan of Bhopal.

5. Tajur Majid.

It is india's largest majid, it comes in Asian ranking too also. The Majid night time illuminated with lights nice to see don't miss it during your visit. It has got big water pool and accommodate lacks of people in its premises at a time. The main majid constructed plingth area itself spreads around 200ft by 300ft distance.

6. Mothi Majid

These two Majid located in heart of old Bhopal called Royal market area. **Other places to See:** 1. Sanchi Buddha Stupi 36Km from Bhopal,2. Peoples Mall just 2 km from Bhopal Main Vegtable market. In this People Mall most of the worlds famous Architect rich structure like Al burj, Taj mehal, etc Miniature model which you can go inside and see in each miniature model in such a size it has been made.

END OF CHAPTER-8

Chapter 9

VISIT TO ODISHA TEMPLES

Odisha historically rich by it s culture and its ruler of Maurya dynasty the King Ashoka. The Bhubhaneshwar, konark and Puri is the Pilgrimage tourist hub. They are all located within 50Km radius. From Bhubaneshwar lot of bus facility available to Konark and Puri. The unexplored beauty and the perfect amalgamation of traditions, culture and art forms in Odisha is amazing that attract tourists from all parts of the world. The main thing to explore in temples is the divinity that you will feel, while another main thing the architecture of the temples of Odisha will keep you mesmerized for a long time

Bhubaneswar

It is known as the City of Temples, where you will find the temples made in an ancient time during 8th to 15 Century AD. During your tour to the capital city of Orissa, Some of the most popular **temples in Bhubaneswar and Odisha** temples include.

Lingaraj Temple:

This temple has got 108 shrines within its premises for different gods. The main shrine is for lord siva. It is the most prominent and must see temple in Bhubaneswar that is dedicated to Harihara – Lord Shiva. It was developed in 11th century A.D. Here the Lingam made in fusion of Lord Siva and hari(Vishnu). This fusion type temple you find very rare.

The main temple has got Garpagirah, Natiya mandapam and entrance hall (Where the food is offered to all the devotees). Here for lord the rice has been offered by temple administration committee in larger volume during afternoon pooja season. Here lingaraj temple hindus only allowed to make pooja inside the temple. The photography strictly prohibited inside the temple complex.

The temple of Lingaraja, the biggest of all at Bhubaneswar is located within a spacious compound wall of left to right measuring 520 feet by 465 feet. The wall is very large in thick and surmounted by a plain slant coping. Lingaraj Temple is a temple of the Hindu god Shiva and is one of the oldest temples of the Temple City Bhubaneswar, a revered pilgrimage centre and the capital of the state of Odisha

Alongside the inner face of the boundary wall there runs a terrace probably meant to protect the compound wall against outside aggression. Bhagavan Lingaraj is half Shiva and half Vishnu. HE is neither worshiped with BEL leaf nor with only TULSI leaf. He is offered with both BEL & TULSI leaf for puja There is one Bow (Dhanush) on top of the temple unlike other Shiv Temple where TRISHUL is placed on top of the other Shiv temples. The Shivalingam in the sanctum of the Lingaraja temple rises to a height of 8 inches above the floor level, and is 8 feet in diameter. The Bhagawati temple is located in the northwest corner of the courtyard. There are several other shrines and temples in this vast courtyard.

History:

Lingaraaj means 'the king of Lingas', 'Linga' or 'Lingam' being the symbol of Lord Shiva worship. The temple is more than 1000 years old, dating back in its present form to the last decade of the eleventh century, though there is evidence that parts of the temple have been there since sixth century AD as the temple has been emphasized in some of the seventh century Sanskrit texts. This is testimony to its sanctity and importance as a Shiva shrine. By the time the Lingaraj temple was constructed, the Jagannath (form of Vishnu) cult had been growing, which historians believe is evidenced by the co-existence of Vishnu and Shiva worship at the temple. Bhubaneshwar the capital of Orissa is a city of temples, several of which are important from an architectural point of view. The Lingaraj temple is the largest of these. It is about a thousand years old.

SIVA TEMPLES IN BHUBANESHWAR

Aisanyesvara Siva Temple- Built in 13thcentury A.D.

Akhadachandi Temple- Built in 10th century A.D.

Bhringesvara Siva Temple-It is in the foothills of Dhauli and left Bank of River Daya.

Champakesvara Siva Temple-Built in 13th century.

Devasabha Temple- Built in 18th century A.D.

Lakhesvara Siva Temple- Built in 13th century AD. It is located very close to renowned Lingaraj Temple.

VISNU TEMPLES IN BHUBANESWAR

Ananta Vasudeva Temple-

Built in 13th century A.D. In the temple, Subhadra and Balram are also worshiped.

MATAJI TEMPLES IN BHUBANESHWAR

Bharati Matha:

It is dedicated to Lord Vishnu and considered as one of the oldest temples in Bhubaneswar.

Gopal Tirtha Matha:

Built in 16th century, it is located in front of the Chitrakarini Temple.

In addition to aforementioned Bhubaneswara Odisha (Orissa) temples, there are also a number of other temples that include Madneswar Siva temple, Mangalesvara Siva temple, Mukteswar Temple, Nagesvara Temple, Pabaneswara temple, Parusurameswar temple, Purvesvara Siva temple, Rajrani Temple, Ram Mandir, Sarvatresvara Siva temple, Sivatirtha Matha, Suka Temple, Svapnesvara Siva temple, Vaital Deula and etc.

In short the famous temples of Bhubaneshwar are Lingaraj temple, Brahmeshwar temple, Mukteshwar temple, Parasurameshwarar temple, Rajarani temple, Vaital deul temple, kedar gowri temple and Iskan temple don't miss it during your visit.

DHAUPURI:

These Dhauligiri **Buddha Stupa** and **Dhaulaswaru** (Lord siva) temple located in small hill lock adjacent to River Daya. At hill hill top you can have panaromic view of Bhubaneshwar outer skirts and river Daya. Just at the foot hill you can find King Ashoka's Rock inscription.

Udayagiri Caves, Khandagiri caves and its Jain temple are main tourist attraction point in Buhbaneshwar. They are very closely located.

In Udyagiri caves you can find double decker cave which is very rare to see and various other caves too available. At hill top you can find the basement of destroyed monuments. From here the bhubaneshwar city panaromic view very nice to see. In Khandagiri hill you can find Maa Barabhuja temple and Jain Adinath temple. The adinath jain temple under renovation when I went the new temple inside work was under progress. This temple near devotees offer their food items to monkeys. They are very dare enough to take food from your hand try during your visit. It is the main tourism hub in Bhubaneswar don't miss it during your visit.

OTHER FAMOUS TEMPLES OF ODISHA

PURI TEMPLES

From Bhubamneshwar only 50 Km distance the world famous Jagannath temple is there. This temple kitchen is Asia's largest kitchen maintained in the temple premises. The world famous chariot festivals carried out here during this period lot of devotees from all over the world gather in lacks. Jagannath means Lord of the Universe.

The main temple is known as Vimana that is nothing but the sanctum enshrining the deity; while the porch or Jagmohana is a place for those who come to pay home to their lords, gods and goddesses. As far as the temples in Odisha are concerned, Vimanas are constructed on a square base and at the same time marked by a curvilinear tower that is called as Shikhara.

The architecture of the temple follows the pattern of many Oriyas temples of the classical period. The main shikhara, or tower, rises above the inner sanctum where the deities installed. Subsidiary shikharas rise above ante-halls. The temple complex is surrounded by a wall, on each side of which is a gopura or gate, over which rises a pyramid-shaped roof. Being the largest temple in the state, it has a complex covering several square blocks with dozens of structures including a mammoth kitchen.

I had visited the temple during charot car festival time lot of people around the world gathered to watch this festival. During this time the Main deities from Jagannath temple shifted to Lord's mousi house for devotees pooja offering purpose at the end of the festival the deities will be shifted to main temple and kept there permanently.

The deities special is made up of Neem tree wood it last life for every 17 years an average life cycle of 17 years once the Dieties were replaced with new one.

MAIN TEMPLE ARCHITECTURE

The main temple structure of this architectural and cultural wonder is 65m (214 feet) high and is built on elevated ground, making it look more imposing. Comprising an area of 10.7 acres, the temple complex is enclosed by two rectangular walls. The outer enclosure is called Meghanada Prachira, 200m (665 ft) by 192m (640 ft). The inner wall is called Kurmabedha, 126m (420 ft) by 95m (315 ft). There are thirty-six traditional communities (Chatisha Niyaga) who render a specific hereditary service to the deities. The temple has as many as 6,000 priests.

There is a wheel on top of the Jagannath Temple made of an alloy of eight metals (asta-dhatu). It is called the Nila Chakra (Blue Wheel), and is 3.5m (11 ft 8 in) high with a circumference of about 11m (36 ft). Every day, a different flag is tied to a mast attached to the Nila Chakra. Every Ekadasi, a lamp is lit on top of the temple near the wheel. There are four gates: the eastern Singhadwara (Lion Gate), the southern Ashwadwara (Horse Gate), the western Vyaghradwara (Tiger Gate), and the northern Hastidwara (Elephant Gate).

There is a carving of each form by the entrance of each gate. The Lion Gate, which is the main gate, is located on Grand Road. Thirty different smaller temples surround the main temple. The Narasimha Temple, adjacent to the western side of the Mukti-mandapa, is said to have been constructed before this temple.

KONARK SUN TEMPLE

It is one of the most popular temples in India that has been witnessing a heavy influx of tourists to india as well as in the state of Odishsa. From Puri to konark mini bus facilty available along the way you can find coastal areas and cashew tree, these total area preserved by forest department of Odisha.

Sun Temple in Konark was built by King Narasimhadeva I in 13th century from oxidized and weathered farraginous sandstone. The erotic sculpture of Sun is the main attraction here; however, the temple compound spread in the area of 261 meter by 160 meter with a 128 feet audience hall. The famous poet Rabindranath tagore who wondered the carvings and sculpture work and descripe as one of the gem of india need to be preserved for ever.

TEMPLE HISTORY

It is believed that the temple was constructed by Samba who was the son of Lord Krishna. As per religious myths, Samba had the problem of leprosy that was brought about by his father's curse on him. And Lord Sun cured him; thus to give them honour, he built **Sun Temple at Konark.**

The renowned temple is very close to shoreline. You can find nice beach and resorts nearby. It is constructed in the form of chariot of Surya that is heavily decorated with stone carving. It looks as if it is stand on wheels. Twelve pairs of ornamented wheels pulled by seven pairs of horses attract tourists and take them back to 13thcentury. The main temple entrance is damaged you can't enter inside, the renovation work going on to polish the rocks and rectify the damaged parts in the main temple during the year 2014.

The temple is opened in early morning when sun rises for Maha Aarati and then closed at 12 in noon. After this it is opened again in evening and closed with sun set. Every year, Danace festival is also organized here that is very popular event in Odisha.

Sri Sri Baladev Jew Temple

This temple is located in Ichhapur in kendrapara Dt. Lord Balabhadra is the main god of this temple. With Balabhadra lord jagannath and Subhadra also worshipped here. Ratana simhasan in the temple Idol of Godess Tulsui in sitting position in there after the sacred seven steps.

Architecture:

This temple spreads around 2 acres of land. This temple has got beautiful garden inside. The boundary wall of temple built at an height of 14 M high. There are four main parts of the temple they are Sri Mandir, Natya Mandir, Bhoga mandap and Mukhashala. The main temple height is 75ft. And width is

40ft bhandar. The main temple has a 7 step construction and heavy baulamalia stone were used for this construction. The main parts of the temples are Garuda Stambha, Ratan bhandar, Snana mandap, Mukti Mandap. The deities of Lord Baladev, lord jagannath and godess Subhadra wera different costumes and are decorated in different forms during importand festive period. This tradition is known as alankara. The rath yatra here is famous for the Brahma taladhwaja rath.

Some Important Alankara are:

Sri Raghunatha Besha on Chaitra Purnima Festival. Padma Besha on Kartik Purnima Festival and Tulsi Vivah in Kartik. Gamhabhisheka Besha – From Shraavana Sukla Dashami to Purnima, holy srinakshatra ceremony of Lord Balarama Pushyabhisheka Besha on Pausha Purnima festival Kanchi Kaveri Besha on Vasant Panchami festival. Suna Besha (Bali Vamana Besha) on Bhadrapad Dwadashi Day Krishna Balarama Besha on Phalguna Purnima festival

Offerings:

There are arrangements for 3 main Naivedya offerings (Dhupa)and 3 minor offerings (Abakasha) for the deities daily. Morning offering (Sakala Dhupa) Offering at pre-noon (Madhhyanna Dhupa) Rice offering (Dwiprahara Dhupa/ Anna Dhupa) Offering at evening (Sandhya Aarati Dhupa) Rice offering (Nisankhudi Dhupa) Offering at night (Badasinghar Dhupa) Different types of offerings (Prasad) are made with trained traditional families, called as Supakara and Mekap are engaged solely for deities. Some of the delicacies are highly patronized in different historic regimes. A comprehensive list of the delicacies is given below. Baula Gaintha, Upana Pitha, Mithei, Chaurashi Vyanjana(84 vegetable Curry), Makara Chaula, Bhaja, Ghia Anna, Dali, Phalamula (fruits), Dry sweets, Ghanavarta, Pura Kakara, Rasabali, Potali Pitha, Chipa Kakara, Karanji, Khaja, Magaja Ladoo, Dalimba, Khuduma,

Nishkudi, Mutha Gaja, Tala, Chhena Chakata are the famous ones.

Baliharchandi Mandira, Near Konark - Puri Road, Puri, Odisha

Panchalingeshwar Temple, Nilagiri, Baleswara, Odisha.

DevKund, Udala, Ambika temple, Devakunda waterfalls, Mayurbhanja, Odisha

Kapilasa Mahadev Temple, Dhenkanal, Odisha

The temples are situated at a height of about 2239 feet from sea level. The main tower of the temple is 60 feet tall. There are two approaches for the temple. One is by climbing 1352 steps and the other is 'Barabanki' or travelling by the twisting way. King Narasinghdeva I of Ganga Dynasty constructed the temple for Sri Chandrasekhar in 1246 A.D as indicated in the Kapilash temple inscription.

In the left side of the temple the 'Payamrta kunda'and in the right side the 'Marichi kunda' exist. The temple has a wooden Jagamohana. Sri Ganesh, Kartikeya, Gangadevi, etc. are found in the temple. Patita pavana Jagannath is installed in the temple as the 'Parsa deva'. Lord Vishwanath temple is also situated in Kapilas. According to some scholars this temple is older than the Chandrasekhar temple, hence it is known as 'Budha linga'. There are many legends about Kapilash pitha and its significance. Tradition describes it as the ashram of Kapila, to some scholars it is the second Kailash of Lord Shiva. Shridhar swami who wrote commentary on Bhagavata Purana stayed there. There are some monasteries in the premises. Maa Tarini is the presiding deity for all Shakti and Tantra peeths or shrines in Orissa. The origin of Shakti or worship of the Earth as a female embodiment of power is found across many cultures all over the world. In Orissa which has a high density of tribal population whose religious practices have been assimilated into the mainstream Hindu faith, the worship of natural formations such as rocks, tree trunks, rivers is widespread among the tribes.

Maa Tarini Temple, Ghatagaon, Keonjhar, Odisha Maa Tarini is always depicted as a red face with two large eyes and a mark in the middle which serves as an indication for a nose and also a tilak.

This primitive conception is symbolic of the simplicity of tribal beliefs and ceremonies. The red colour has been attributed to dyes made out of iron ores or ocher which are quite plentiful in the state and would thus have been used by the tribes for anointing and decorating the sacred figures of worship.

The ornate letters in the background mean "Maa" or Mother in the Oriya language. They were a much later addition although the Oriya script did change very slightly over the millennia. In this form she is very similar to the conception of the Goddess Kali at Kalighat. Although the two are embodiments of the same divinity, Kali is the Goddess of death and destruction whereas Maa Tarini is the force of life. Interestingly, two of the names of Kali are Maa Taara and Tara Tarini.

BOLANGIR DISTRICT

Jharial- Chausathi Jogini Temple together with three minors shrines.

CUTTACK DISTRICT

1. Bandareswar-Ruins of the Buddhist Temples and images
2. Chandia-Hill containing many valuable sculptures, images and inscriptions, etc., of Buddhistic age. On the top, there is a Math and a small Temple of mahakal.
3. Lalitgiri-Ruins of Buddhist Temple and images
4. Ratnagiri-Hills containing many valuable sculptures and Temple images
5. Simhanatha Pitha- Mauza Simhanatha Mahadeva Temple
6. Gopinathpur-Magura.

7. Dhanmandal- Pancha Pandava Temple
8. Rameswar-Durga Temple

DHENKANAL DISTRICT

1. Bajrakot-Bighneswara Mahadeva Temple
2. Kualo-Swapaneswar Temple.

GANJAM DISTRICT

1. Kottakolla-Gangadharswami Temple
2. Jagadiswarswami Temple
3. Mahendragiri-Bhima Temple
4. Kunti Temple
5. Yudhisthira Temple.
6. Paralakhemundi-Hanuman Temple
7. Badagaon-Group of Siva Temple
8. Jirabadi (Near Bhanjanagar)
9. Ramapada Temple.

PHULBANI DISTRICT

1. Gandharadhi-Temples of Nilamadhava and Sidheswara
2. Baudha Town-Paschima Somanatha, Bhubaneswar and Kapileswar

Temples.

BHUBANESHWAR

Lord Lingaraj Temple with all the minor temples in the compound namely

1. Amania Well
2. Astamurti
3. Chandeswar Deb
4. Gopaluni Temple

5. Ladukeswar Temple
6. Parvati Temple
7. Sabitri Devi Temple
8. Sakreswar Temple
9. Sathidevi Temple 9. Sisiresvara Temple

Other temple in Buhbaneshwar.

10. Maitreswar Temple with all the minor temples in the compound
11. Makareswar Temple with its minor shrines
12. Markandeswar Temple
13. Mukteswar Temple with its shrines but excluding the Murich Kunda
14. Parsurameswar Temple
15. Raja Rani Temple
16. Sari Temple
17. Sidheswar Temple

Hirapur

Chausathi Yogini Temple known as Mahamaya Temple

Raghunathpur (Banpur)

Daksha Prajapati Temple

Chourasi-Varahi Temple

BALASORE DISTRICT

1. Guamala-Kumareswar Temple
2. Aredi-Akhandalamani Temple
3. Palia-Biranchinarayan Temple
4. Near Tihidi-Dapanayakani Temple
5. Haripur-Satabhauni Temple
6. Bhadrak-Bhadrakali Temple
7. Avana-Brahmani Temple
8. Gaurangpur-Gouranga Temple

9. Ramakrishnapur-Rameswar Temple
10. Rahandia-Rameswar Temple
11. Bodaka-Nahakani Temple

BALANGIR DISTRICT

1. Vaidyanath Kosaleswara Temple
2. Ranipur Jharial -Indralath Temple
3. Ranipur Jharial-Somesvara Temple

KEONJHAR DISTRICT

1. Deogaon-Kosaleswar Temple
2. Keonjhargarh-Baladeva Jew Temple.

KALAHANDI DISTRICT

1. Khariar-Dadhibaman Temple
2. Budhikomna-Patalesvara Temple
3. Komna-Jagannath Temple
4. Khariar-Raktambari Temple.

KORAPUT DISTRICT

1. Paikapada-Pataleswar group of Temples
2. Jogamunda Hill (Padmapur)

Mallikeswar and Nilakantheswar Temple

3. Boriguma-Bhairava Temple
4. Nandapur-Ganesha Temple
5. Nandapur-Bhairavi Temple (Group of Temples)
6. Nandapur-Sarveswara Temple

MAYURBHANJ DISTRICT

1. Khiching-Khichakesvari Temple
2. Rairangapur-Isanesvara Temple

PURI DISTRICT

1. Bhubaneswar-Swarnajaleswar Temple
2. Algum-Gatiswar Temple
3. Dhauli-Bahirangeswar Temple
4. Chaurasi-Laxminarayan Temple
5. Amareswar-Amareswar Temple
6. Bishnupur-Somanath Temple
7. Dhauli-Dhabaleswar Temple
8. Bhubaneswar- Satrughneswar-Bharateswar and Laxmaneswar Temples.
9. Balisahi-Javan Haridas Temple.
10. Birabhadrapur-Somanath Temple
11. Chandeswar-Chandeswar Temple
12. Bayalisabati (near Gop)-Gangeswari Temple
13. Barisha-Ramachandi Temple
14. Kenduli-Chandi Temple
15. Jiunti-Iswaradeva Temple
16. Nairi-Harihara Dev Temple
17. Samantarapur-Dakshineswar Temple
18. Kakatapur-Mangala Temple
19. Garadipanchana-Buddhanath Temple
20. Brahmagiri Allarnath Temple
21. Prataparudrapur-Akhandaleswar Temple.
22. Kakudia-Gopinath Temple
23. Sakhigopal-Sakhigopal Temple
24. Lingaraj temple
25. Dhauli-Sidha Ganesha Temple
26. Banapur-Bhagabati Temple
27. Bhubaneswar-Mohini Temple
28. Bhubaneswar-Dwarabasini Temple
29. Bhubaneswar-Bhawani Sankar Temple
30. Patia-Killa-Sikhara Chandi Temple
31. Kantilo-Nilamadhava Temple
32. Rameswar-Ramanidhi Dev Temple
33. Rameswar-Jagatramohana Temple1Baragarh (Bhubaneswar)
34. Banpur (reserve forest)-Bankadagarh Siva Temple
35. Sauria-Bani Vakreswara Temple
36. Ghoradia-Somanath Temple

37. Kalyanapur-Laxmi Nrasimha Temple
38. Lataharana-Grameswara Temple
39. Budhapada-Somanath Temple
40. Barimunda-Lakheswara Temple
41. Raktapatta-Kunjabehari Temple
42. Bhubaneswar-Bibhisaneswar Temple
43. Sarakana-Gopinath Temple
44. Kurala-Chandeswar Temple
45. Bhaskareswar Temple.
46. Brahmeswar Temple with its minor shrine in the compound
47. Nabakeswar Temple
48. Rameswar Temple.
49. Besuaghai-Magheswar Temple with its minor shrine.

SAMBALPUR DISTRICT

1. Paikamala-Nrusimhanath Temple.

END OF CHAPTER- 9

Chapter 10

MAHARASTRA TEMPLE

It accommodates indias business capital city Mumbai. The state is historically rich and famous for sculpture work. Every where in the state is to be found evidence of the artistic skills of a people whose culture goes back thousands of yesrs in song and dance, in painting and sculpture, in architects and handicrafts. It has got world famous and hertitage cave temples like Ajanta and Ellora caves near Aurangabad. All over the Maharastra the relices of the glorious history, the great warrior like Chatrapathi Shivaji's massive forts on hill top and historic battle sites all tell the story of aGreat nations rise from division to unity.

MUMBAI TEMPLES

1. Elephanta caves
2. Mahalakshmi temple
3. Jogesrwari cave temple
4. Virar lord siva temple
5. Iskan temple
6. Siddi vinayak temple
7. Ambarnath temple near kalian
8. Titwala ganesha temple 75Km from mumbai

PUNE TEMPLE

1. Parvathi temple on hill top
2. Siddi vinayak temple in main bazzar
3. Osho ashram
4. Pataleshwar caves
5. Lonavala and kandala cave temples.
6. WAI Ganapathi temple and buddist lonara caves temple

NASHIK TEMPLE

Indian currency were printed here and it is called as Mini kasi, it accommodates most of the old temples in Panchavadi in the banks Godavari river.

- Panchavadi where lakshmana reka where sita has been abducted by ravana, other temples closely located here are sita kund, ram kund, kala ram, Ghora ram, Bhakthi dam, Mukthidam, seet gupha, shiv mandir, kapaleshwar Mandir.
- kapila Godavari sangamam and pundulana caves in mahendravadi hills.
- Balaji mandir and someshwar mandir where boating facility available in river Godavari. From nashik 70Km to Shridi from Shridi 60Km to ellora caves.

AURANGABAD TEMPLE

1. Ajanta and ellora caves
2. Gushmeshwar jothrlingam
3. Aurangabad cave temples
4. Pitalkhora caves dates back to 300 B.C
5. Shanni Shingnapur temple 92Km from Aurangabad and 30Km from shridi saibaba temple.

KOLHAPUR TEMPLE

This is erstwhile capital of olden Maratha state is have some splendid palaces and royal homes. It is also known as Dhakshina kasi as the temples here are considred as most important in Maharastra. The famous Mahalakshmi temple built in 7th century is the fine example Hemadpanti style architecture and its adorned with inticate carvings. The main sanctum enshrines a 40 Kg idol of the Goddess Mahalakshmi, it is belived this idol is Suambu(Naturally formed). This shrine has been decorated with a primeval monolith of uncut diamonds and precious stones. From belgam air port 105 Km to kolaphur. From Mumbai also good bus facilty available.

This state accommodates **Five jothilingam** status temple for this package tours and travels operator available from all major cities. 1. Tryambakeshwar 2. Gushmeshwarar 3. Aundha Nagnath 4. Bhimasankar 5. Paril Vaijnath.

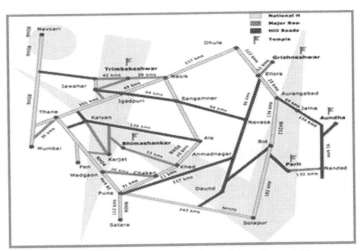

Pancha Jothirlingam and Asht vinayak temple road Map.

It also have Asht(8 Nos) vinayak temple as follow, for this package tours and travels operator available from all major cities.

TOWN	LORD NAME	DISATNACE FROM PUNE
1. Morgaon	Shri Moreshwarji	79 Km
2. Theur	Shri Chintamani	25 Km
3. Siddhatek	Shri siddivinayak	99 Km
4. Ranjangaon	Shri Mahaganapathi	53 Km
5. Lenyadri	Shri Girijatmaj vinayak	90 Km
6. Ojhar	Shri Vigneshwar	85 Km
7. Pali	Shri Ballaeshwar	111 Km.
8. Mahad	Shri Varad Vinayak	75 Km.

END OF CHAPTER 10

References

1. Hindu temples-by swami harshananda.
2. Tourist guide of Tamilnadu.
3. Valzipadu isthalangal.
4. Kombakonam kovilkal-By Vijaya Sharma.
5. 108 Siva isthalangal-By Nagerkovil Krishnan.
6. Tamilazka thirukovilkal-By Pugali Bharath
7. Jothirlingam -by Jabalpur Nagaraj
8. Jothir lingam-Websites.
9. Direct temple visits reference from temples inscription.
10. Tourist guide of Maharastra.
11. CBSE social science Text book of sixth standard.
12. Andhravil Sivan-By Siva sundaram
13. My own website www.templedynamic.blogspot.com.

1. Somanathar 2. Mallikaarjunur 3. Mahakalar 4. Omkareshwar 5. Vaithyanath 6. Bhimasankar 7. Rameshwar 8. Nageshwar 9. Kasiviswanathar 10. Tryambakeshwar 11. Kedernath 12. Grishneshwar or Kushmeshwarar.

In this book I attempt to explain about Sivam legend Lord Siva's oldest HOLY shrines of Dwarthasa Jothir lingam temples. Based on my own visit to this temple I explained the present fact and facility available, History of the temple, Route guide to the temple and sculpture work. I would like to thank almighty for HIS blessing to write this book.